Fundamental
Computer Concepts

Fundamental Computer Concepts

William S. Davis
Miami University
Oxford, Ohio

ADDISON-WESLEY PUBLISHING COMPANY
Reading, Massachusetts • Menlo Park, California
Don Mills, Ontario • Wokingham, England
Amsterdam • Sydney • Singapore
Tokyo • Madrid • Bogotá
Santiago • San Juan

Sponsoring Editor:	Mark S. Dalton	
Production Supervisor:	Mary K. Coffey	
Text Design:	To-The-Point	
Illustrator:	Textbook Art Associates	
Production Coordinators:	Helen Wythe	
	Ezra C. Holston	
Cover Design:	Marshall Henrichs	

Library of Congress Cataloging-in-Publication Data

Davis, William S., 1943–
  Fundamental computer concepts.

  Includes index.
  1. Computers.   I. Title.
QA76.D3333155 1986   004   85-26881
ISBN 0–201–11305–8

Credits:
From W.S. Davis, *True Basic Primer,* Addison-Wesley, 1986: Figures 1.4, 3.1, 3.4, and 3.6.
From W.S. Davis, *Computers and Business Information Processing,* second edition, Addison-Wesley, 1983: Figures
  2.6, 3.12, 3.13, 3.15, 3.16, 4.7, 4.9, 9.2, 10.13, and 11.8.
From W.S. Davis, *Information Processing Systems,* Addison Wesley, 1981: Figure 10.14.
From W.S. Davis, *The NECEN Voyage,* Addison-Wesley, 1985: Figure 4.2.

EFGHIJ-HA-8987

Preface

Clearly, computers have become our "tool for modern times," and more and more people want to learn something about them. For many, the objective is simply understanding basic concepts. Engineers, business people, scientists, mathematicians, and students in these disciplines recognize the computer as an important professional tool, and thus need more intensive training. Computer professionals and students majoring in computer-related fields must, of course, study computers in considerable depth. To complicate matters, a course designed for business students will differ from a similar course intended for engineers, or computer scientists, or liberal arts majors. Thus our schools teach a variety of introductory computer courses.

Though different, most of these courses share a common set of fundamental concepts. For many students, these basic concepts are enough. The science, engineering, business, or mathematics student builds on them to quickly grasp computer applications in his or her field. For students in computer-related disciplines, these same concepts provide a solid foundation for future studies, but the underlying, fundamental concepts are the same, no matter what the course's orientation.

Many introductory courses supplement these fundamental concepts with other topics. Some stress social implications. Others teach a programming language, or introduce students to computer applications in a particular field. Numerous excellent, inexpensive books are available for most popular programming languages and application packages. Used in conjunction with a low-cost computer concepts text, they could support almost any introductory computer course.

That's the basic idea behind *Fundamental Computer Concepts*. It's designed to be a technically accurate, technically complete, brief, clearly written, inexpensive introduction to computers. Used alone, in conjunction with outside readings, or to supplement a programming or application package text, it can form a solid base for a variety of introductory computer courses. I hope you find it both interesting and informative.

Acknowledgments

The manuscript for *Fundamental Computer Concepts* was prepared by Venis Torge. Dr. Allison McCormack copy edited the manuscript and made many valuable suggestions. The efforts of Mark Dalton, Katherine Harutunian, and Mary Coffey, all of Addison-Wesley Publishing Company, and Joyce T. Snow, an independent editorial consultant, were invaluable. Stephanie Grand, of Oxford, Ohio, took the photographs that appear as Figures 1.8 and 2.1. Finally, the author would like to acknowledge the contributions of four reviewers: Robert Schuerman of Cal Poly State University in San Luis Obispo, California; Paul H. Cheney of the University of Georgia in Athens, Georgia; W. James Abbott, Jr., of Broome Community College in Binghamton, New York; and Alistair D.C. Holden, of the University of Washington in Seattle, Washington.

WSD
Oxford, Ohio

Contents

Fundamental
Computer Concepts

1.

Computers: Getting Started

What Is a Computer?

Data and Information

A **computer** is a machine whose function is to accept **data** and process them into **information**. Data are facts or observations, while information is the meaning we attribute to them.

Let's use an example to illustrate. A medieval astronomer, Tycho Brahe, spent his entire adult life observing and recording the positions of the planets. He collected data: on a given night, Mars occupied a given position in the sky. He recorded volumes of such data, but was never quite sure what they meant.

His successor, Johannes Kepler, sensed a pattern: the orbit of Mars resembled an ellipse. He spent much of his life processing Brahe's data, performing tedious computations and reorganizing the observations in an attempt to verify that pattern. Eventually he succeeded, publishing his laws of planetary motion in 1621.

Kepler's laws represent information. Using them, he could understand and predict the motions of the planets. Scientists and engineers still rely on his laws to help plan space flights. Information has meaning.

Clearly, Kepler's laws were derived from Brahe's data, but the raw data were useless without processing. Until they were organized and the necessary calculations performed, the data were unstructured facts, with no clear meaning. Knowing the exact position of Mars on April 1, 1599, might earn an extra move in Trivial Pursuit, but, by itself, that fact is not very useful. Processing data extracts their meaning.

Data Processing

A **computer** is a data processing machine. Data flow into the machine as **input** (*Fig. 1.1*). Information flows from the machine as **output**. The computer processes the data. Johannes Kepler spent twenty years of his life processing data. Today, a college student using a computer can repeat his computations in a few *hours*.

Fig. 1.1   A computer is a machine that processes data into information. It accepts input data, processes these data, and generates information as output.

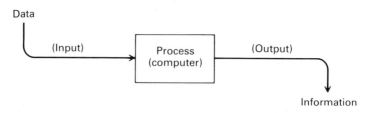

What do we mean when we say that a computer processes data? We process iron ore to make steel; we process wood pulp to make paper. "Process" implies that a change takes place, that the raw materials are in some way restructured or manipulated. Often, *data* processing involves filtering and summarizing data so that underlying patterns can be perceived. How does a computer process its data? What functions, what operations, can it perform? Generally, computers can add, subtract, multiply, divide, compare, copy, request input, and request output. So can most pocket calculators. What makes a computer different?

The Stored Program Concept

To add two numbers on a calculator, you:

1. Enter the first number.
2. Press the add (+) button.
3. Enter the second number.
4. Press the result (=) button.
5. Record the sum for future reference.

The calculator finds the sum, but *you* must provide control by deciding what button to push next. A calculator requires direct human intervention at each step.

A computer processes data automatically, without human intervention. Computers are *not* intelligent, however. They don't know when to add, or subtract, or compare, or request input. If a computer is to function without direct human control, it must be given a set of instructions to guide it, step by step, through a process. The set of instructions is called a **program**. The program is stored physically inside the machine, making it a **stored program** (*Fig. 1.2*). The stored program distinguishes a computer from a calculator and allows it to function without human intervention. Let's incorporate this idea into our definition:

Computer: **A machine that processes data into information under the control of a stored program.**

Fig. 1.2 A computer processes data automatically under control of a stored program.

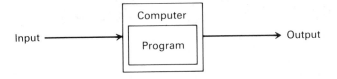

A Computer System

System Components

A computer system consists of several basic components (*Fig. 1.3*). An input device provides data. The data are stored in **memory**, which also holds a program. Under control of that program the computer's **processor** manipulates the data, storing the results back into memory. Finally, the results flow from the computer to an output device. Additionally, most modern computers use secondary storage to extend memory capacity.

Fig. 1.3   A computer system consists of four basic components: an input device, an output device, main memory, and a processor. Secondary storage is often used to extend memory capacity.

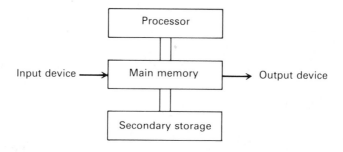

Fig. 1.4   A typical computer system. Input is provided by a keyboard. Output goes to the screen or to the printer. The processor and main memory are located inside the cabinet. The disk drives provide secondary storage.

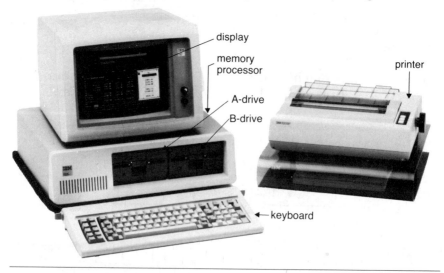

Consider the computer system pictured in *Fig. 1.4*. In the foreground, the keyboard is an input device. Above the keyboard is an output device, the display screen. The image displayed on a screen is temporary; a more permanent copy of the output can be obtained by sending it to a printer. The computer's processor and main memory are located in the small cabinet near the center of the picture. The diskette drives in the front of the cabinet extend the computer's memory; programs often enter the system through such secondary storage devices.

The basic building block of a modern computer is a chip (*Fig. 1.5*), a complex, integrated electronic circuit etched on a tiny square of silicon no bigger than a fingernail. Since loose chips are fragile and difficult to handle, they are normally packaged (*Fig. 1.6*), and mounted on boards (*Fig. 1.7*). A computer is assembled by sliding the appropriate boards into a cabinet (*Fig. 1.8*). One board might hold the processor. Another might hold main memory, while a third might contain the electronics to link a particular input or output device to the system.

Fig. 1.5   The basic building block of a modern computer is a chip.

AT&T Bell Laboratories

Fig. 1.6   Chips are fragile and difficult to handle. Thus they are packaged on carriers before they are used.

Fairchild Camera and Instrument Corporation

Fig. 1.7 The major components of a computer consist of a number of chips mounted on a board.

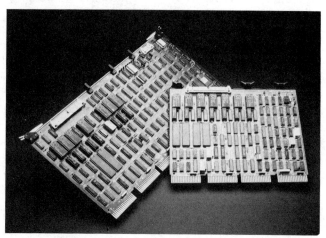

Plessey Peripheral Systems, Irvine, California

Fig. 1.8 A computer is assembled by sliding the appropriate boards into a cabinet.

How a Computer Works

Let's use the system pictured in *Fig. 1.9* to illustrate how a typical computer works. A computer is controlled by a stored program; thus, the first step in using the machine is copying the program from diskette into memory (*Fig. 1.10a*). Now, the processor can begin executing instructions. Input data from the keyboard are stored in memory (*Fig. 1.10b*). The processor manipulates the data, storing the results back into memory (*Fig. 1.10c*). Finally, the results are output (*Fig. 1.10d*).

Fig. 1.9 We'll use this diagram of a typical system to illustrate how a computer works.

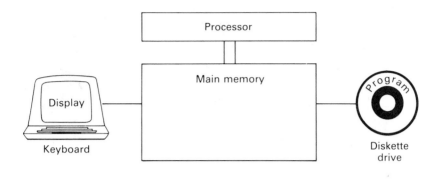

Fig. 1.10 This series of drawings illustrates how a computer works.

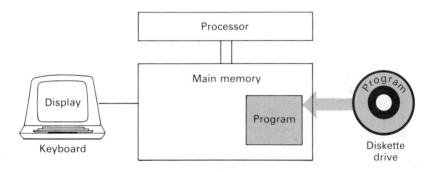

a. A program is copied from disk and stored in memory.

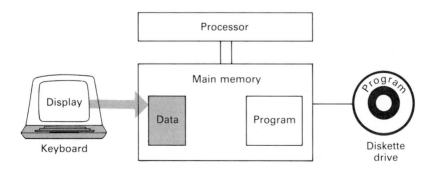

b. Under control of the stored program, data are read from the keyboard and stored in memory.

Fig. 1.10

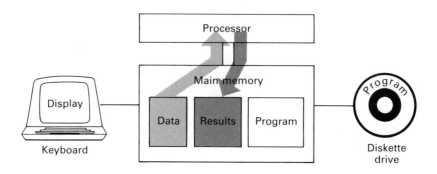

c. The processor manipulates the data, storing the results back in memory.

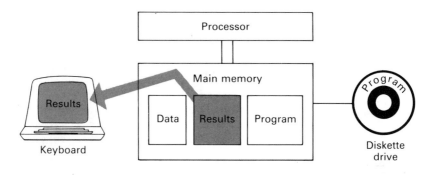

d. Finally, the results are output.

Memory's contents are easy to change. Thus, when one set of data has been processed, the program can be repeated, reading and processing new data, and generating new output. If the data can be changed, why not the program? When a program is finished, a new one can take its place in memory, allowing the computer to process completely different data. One minute it can generate paychecks from labor data under control of a payroll program. The next minute, it can prepare bills from invoices under control of a billing program. Later, this same collection of components, controlled by yet another program, can read statistical data and produce a bar chart, or sense the movements of a joystick and manipulate the position of an imaginary spaceship on a display screen.

The physical components of a computer—the processor, memory, input devices, and output devices—are its **hardware**. You can see them, touch them, and feel them. Programs and data are different, existing only as electronic pulses stored in memory. **Software** is a general term for programs.

A Plan of Attack

At this point, you should have a basic sense of the functions of the processor, main memory, input devices, output devices, and secondary storage, and should know that a computer processes data into information under the control of a program. Over the next several chapters, we'll discuss each major component in more detail, beginning with the computer itself. Once we've covered the components, we'll consider how they are assembled to form complete computer systems. To help you check your understanding, each chapter ends with a brief self-test.

As you study the processor, or memory, or input devices, or software, don't lose sight of the fact that a computer is a collection of components, each of which must do its part. The basic purpose of this first chapter was to give you a high-level overview of a complete computer system. As you read the next several chapters, you will encounter a great deal of technical detail, and it's easy to "miss the forest for the trees." As you read, use the material in this chapter as a framework.

Key Words

At the end of each chapter, you'll find a list of keywords. You should know what these words mean; if you don't, you've missed something, and should reread the material. After defining each term in your own words, check your answers against the glossary.

- computer
- data
- hardware
- information

- input
- memory
- output
- processor

- program
- software
- stored program

Self-Test

At the end of each chapter, you'll find a brief self-test. The intent of these objective questions is to let you check your understanding of the basic terms and concepts introduced in the chapter. Answer the questions, and then compare your responses to the key. If you miss a question, review the associated material. If you miss more than two or three, it might be a good idea to reread the chapter.

1. Unstructured facts.

   a. information
   b. data

   c. bytes
   d. processes

2. The meaning that human beings attribute to facts.

   a. information   c. knowledge
   b. data   d. structure

3. A computer processes _____ into _____ .

   a. information/data   c. facts/data
   b. data/information   d. information/facts

4. Data flow into the computer as _____ .

   a. output   c. a process
   b. a program   d. input

5. Information flows from a computer as _____ .

   a. output   c. a program
   b. memory   d. input

6. The _____ distinguishes a computer from a calculator.

   a. processor   c. memory
   b. stored program   d. output

7. Data and program instructions are stored in _____ .

   a. the processor   c. the stored program
   b. an output device   d. memory

8. The computer component that actually manipulates the data is _____.

   a. main memory   c. the processor
   b. an input device   d. an output device

9. The basic building block of a modern computer is a _____ .

   a. chip   c. transistor
   b. tube   d. switch

10. Chips are normally mounted on _____ . Typically, each one contains the electronics for one of the computer's major components.

   a. plates   c. cylinders
   b. boards   d. carriers

11. The physical components of a computer are collectively called
    _____ .

    a. peripherals   c. boards
    b. software   d. hardware

12. Programs are known collectively as _____ .

    a. secondary storage   c. stored programs
    b. software   d. hardware

Answers

1.b 2.a 3.b 4.d 5.a 6.b 7.d 8.c 9.a 10.b 11.d 12.b

Relating the Concepts

There is more to understanding computer concepts than knowing the meanings of a few key terms. Thus, following the objective self-test, each chapter ends with a series of more subjective and thought-provoking questions. Many of these questions will ask you to explain a concept, explain why a computer works the way it does, or relate two or more concepts. Others will force you to link concepts presented in two or more chapters. Still others will ask you to extrapolate from the material presented in this book. No answers are suggested. If you find one or more questions a mystery, reread the material. If you still can't answer them, ask for help.

1. Distinguish between data and information.

2. Relate the terms data and information to the terms input and output.

3. A stored program distinguishes a computer from a calculator. Explain.

4. What is a computer? Don't just reproduce the definition; explain what each technical term in the definition means.

5. Draw a sketch showing the primary components of a typical computer system. Briefly explain what each component does.

6. Explain the difference between hardware and software.

7. Briefly explain a computer's basic input/process/output cycle.

2.

The Processor and Main Memory

KEY CONCEPTS

Inside a computer

The binary number system

Main memory
- Physical storage devices
- Bytes, words, and addresses
- Addressing memory
- Reading and writing memory

The processor
- Machine cycles

Inside a Computer

In Chapter 1, we studied the input/process/output cycle. We saw how both data and programs are stored in main memory and, under control of a stored program, how a processor converts raw data to information. The intent was to provide you with an overview of a computer system.

The next step is to analyze the individual components in more detail. We'll begin with the computer itself. If we take the cover off a small computer and look inside (*Fig. 2.1*), we'll see a few circuit boards, some cables, and some wires. The real computer lies within the circuitry on those boards. Let's zero in for a closer look. Before we do, however, we should briefly consider the "language" of a computer: binary.

The Binary Number System

A computer is an electronic device that operates on precisely timed pulses of electric current. The processor reacts to pulse and no pulse patterns. Memory holds these on/off patterns. The **binary** number system is ideal for representing such patterns because it uses only two symbols: 0 and 1.

Exactly what is the binary number system? Generally, a number system is a scheme for representing numeric values. In the decimal system, we use combinations of ten symbols, 0 through 9. The digits alone are not enough, however; their relative positions are also important. For example, we know that 03 is three and 30 is thirty because of the digit 3's relative position. Each position has a value. The positional values (1, 10, 100, 1000) are factors of ten. The value of a number is determined by multiplying each digit by its positional value and then adding these products (*Fig. 2.2*).

Fig. 2.1   A computer is constructed from a few circuit boards.

Fig. 2.2 In the decimal number system, positional values are factors of ten. To find the value of any number, multiply each digit by its positional value and add the products.

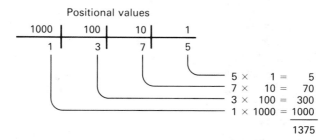

In the binary number system, the positional values are factors of two — 1, 2, 4, 8, 16, ... (*Fig. 2.3*). Only two symbols are needed: 0 and 1. The "digit-times-place-value" rule still holds, however; to find the value of any number, multiply each digit by its place or positional value, and add the products. Thus, as you can see in Fig. 2.3, the binary number 10 is equivalent to the decimal number 2, while 101 is equivalent to the decimal number 5.

We use decimal numbers because we find them convenient (probably because we have ten fingers). A computer uses binary numbers because it finds binary convenient. A binary digit, or **bit**, is the basic unit of storage on a computer. Physical storage devices hold bits, and processors manipulate bits. A computer is a binary machine.

For most readers, a basic sense of the binary number system is enough. Others, in particular students who plan to major in a computer-related discipline, may require more depth. The Appendix presents additional details on number systems, data formats, and codes.

Fig. 2.3 In the binary number system, positional values are factors of two. The "digit-times-place-value" rule still works.

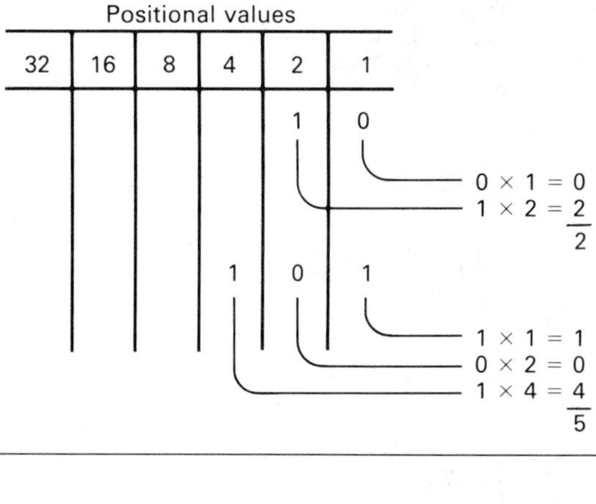

Positional values

32	16	8	4	2	1

$$0 \times 1 = 0$$
$$1 \times 2 = 2$$
$$\overline{2}$$

$$1 \times 1 = 1$$
$$0 \times 2 = 0$$
$$1 \times 4 = 4$$
$$\overline{5}$$

Main Memory

Physical Storage Devices

Consider the bank of switches and light bulbs pictured in *Fig. 2.4.* Each switch is a simple mechanical device that can assume either of two states — on or off. Let's set the switches. Now, we'll supply an electric current. Which bulbs light? Obviously, only those controlled by the switches we set on. If we repeat the experiment, the same bulbs light. If we change the switch settings, different bulbs light. The switch is an elementary storage or memory device, with "on" representing a 1-bit, and "off," a 0-bit.

Carefully distinguish between the physical device (the switch) and its value (0 or 1). The switch is hardware; its setting represents software or data. The value is easy to change — just flip the switch. The value, the software or data, is not permanent; the hardware (the switch) is.

Any device that can assume and hold either of two states is a potential computer storage device. Most modern computers use **integrated circuit memory** (*Fig. 2.5*). A small computer might contain enough memory to store thousands of bits; a large machine might store millions. The difference is one of degree, not function.

Fig. 2.4   A light switch is a simple example of a storage or memory device.

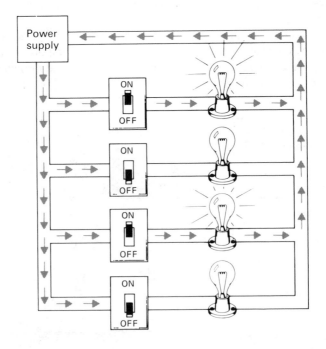

Fig. 2.5 A typical integrated circuit memory board.

Bytes and Words

A single bit can hold either a 0 or a 1. Generally, however, the contents of memory are envisioned as groups of bits rather than as individual bits (for the same reasons we focus on words and sentences rather than individual letters when we read a novel). Although the bit is still the basic unit of storage, computers normally manipulate bytes or words.

A **byte** contains enough bits (usually eight) to represent a single character. Two binary codes, ASCII (the American Standard Code for Information Interchange) and EBCDIC (the Extended Binary Coded Decimal Interchange Code) are commonly used to represent characters inside a computer (*Fig. 2.6*). For example, a capital A, in ASCII, is 01000001. Within main memory, a single byte (eight bits) would hold that bit pattern. In general, each byte holds a single coded character (letter, digit, or punctuation mark).

Bytes are fine for storing characters, but are too small to hold a meaningful number. Most computers are able to manipulate a group of bytes called a **word**. Some small computers have 8-bit words. Other, more powerful machines work with 16-bit (2-byte), 32-bit (4-byte), and even 64-bit words. Thus we have a memory hierarchy (*Fig. 2.7*). The basic unit of storage is the bit. Bits are grouped to form bytes, which, in turn, are grouped to form words. In one application, a given word might be used to hold a binary number. In another, that word's bytes might hold individual characters, or a program instruction.

Fig. 2.6 The ASCII and EBCDIC codes are often used to represent characters inside a computer. Other bit patterns not shown are used to represent punctuation marks and other special symbols.

Character	EBCDIC	ASCII-8
A	1100 0001	0100 0001
B	1100 0010	0100 0010
C	1100 0011	0100 0011
D	1100 0100	0100 0100
E	1100 0101	0100 0101
F	1100 0110	0100 0110
G	1100 0111	0100 0111
H	1100 1000	0100 1000
I	1100 1001	0100 1001
J	1101 0001	0100 1010
K	1101 0010	0100 1011
L	1101 0011	0100 1100
M	1101 0100	0100 1101
N	1101 0101	0100 1110
O	1101 0110	0100 1111
P	1101 0111	0101 0000
Q	1101 1000	0101 0001
R	1101 1001	0101 0010
S	1110 0010	0101 0011
T	1110 0011	0101 0100
U	1110 0100	0101 0101
V	1110 0101	0101 0110
W	1110 0110	0101 0111
X	1110 0111	0101 1000
Y	1110 1000	0101 1001
Z	1110 1001	0101 1010
0	1111 0000	0011 0000
1	1111 0001	0011 0001
2	1111 0010	0011 0010
3	1111 0011	0011 0011
4	1111 0100	0011 0100
5	1111 0101	0011 0101
6	1111 0110	0011 0110
7	1111 0111	0011 0111
8	1111 1000	0011 1000
9	1111 1001	0011 1001

Fig. 2.7 In a computer's main memory, bits are combined to form bytes, and bytes, in turn, are combined to form words. In this example, we have pictured a 32-bit or 4-byte word.

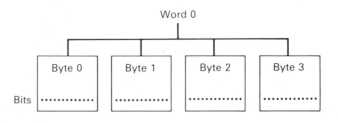

It's important to note that character data and numeric data are different. Characters are represented by a code. Each one is independent. The concept of positional value is irrelevant; multiplying each digit by its positional value and then adding the products produces a meaningless result. In contrast, the bits that form a number are coded in specific relative positions, each of which has a positional value — 1, 2, 4, 8, and so on. The "digit-times-place-value" rule works with numbers, but not with characters. (See the Appendix for more details.)

Addressing Memory

A typical microcomputer contains 128,000 (128K*) or more bytes or words, while a large mainframe may have millions! A given element of data might be stored in any one of them. If the processor needs a particular data element, how does it find the byte or word that holds it?

Each physical storage unit is assigned a unique **address**. On most computers, the bytes or words are numbered sequentially — 0, 1, 2, and so on. The processor accesses a specific memory location by referencing its address. For example, if the processor needs the data stored in byte 1048, it asks memory for the contents of byte 1048. Since there is only one byte 1048, the processor gets the right data. Depending on the computer, bytes or words are the basic *addressable* units of memory. Data move between the processor and main memory a byte or a word at a time.

Reading and Writing Memory

A location in **main memory** is accessed by its address. Often, the contents of memory are simply read. When memory is read, its contents are not changed. For example, imagine that byte number 42 contains the character A. If the processor reads byte 42, the A is still there. However, writing to main memory destroys the old contents. If the processor were to write the character X to byte 42, the new value would replace the old, and the A would be lost forever.

The main memory of most computers is composed of random access memory, or **RAM**. The programmer (through a program, of course) can read or write RAM. Input data can be stored in RAM, destroying the old contents of the selected bytes or words. Once the data are in, they can be read and manipulated by the processor, and results written to other memory locations. Finally, the contents can be sent to an output device. When a program is finished, a new program can be copied into RAM, erasing the old one in the process. The contents of RAM are easy to change.

---

* Technically, the suffix K, which stands for kilo, means 1024. Thus, a computer with 128K bytes of memory contains 131,072 actual memory locations.

Usually, RAM's flexibility is an advantage. Occasionally, however, it can be a problem. Consider, for example, the automatic teller terminals used in many banks. They are controlled by small computers which, in turn, are controlled by programs. A sharp programmer might be able to modify one of those programs to give free access to certain accounts. Needless to say, the bank could not tolerate such changes. The bank needs a program that can be read by the processor, but not modified. Such programs are stored in read-only memory, or **ROM**. Another good example of a ROM-based program is the BASIC language interpreter found in many microcomputers; we'll discuss interpreters in Chapter 7. As the name implies, ROM is "permanent" memory that can be read, but not written.

The Processor

The **processor**, often called the **central processing unit (CPU)** or **main processor**, is the component that processes or manipulates data. A processor can do nothing without a program to provide control; whatever intelligence a computer has is derived from software, not hardware. The processor manipulates data stored in main memory under the control of a program stored in main memory.

Fig. 2.8   An instruction is composed of an operation code and one or more operands. The operation code tells the computers what to do. The operand or operands identify the addresses of the data elements to be manipulated.

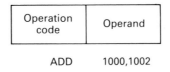

Fig. 2.9   A processor contains four key components.

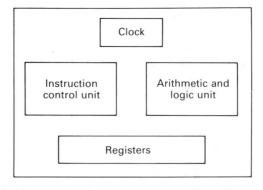

The processor is controlled by a program. A program consists of a series of **instructions**. Each instruction is a group of bits that tells the computer to perform one of its basic functions: add, subtract, multiply, divide, compare, copy, start input, or start output. Each instruction consists of two parts, an **operation code** and one or more **operands** (*Fig. 2.8*). The operation code tells the computer what to do (for example, add, subtract, compare), and the operands identify the memory locations that will participate in the operation. For example, the instruction in *Fig. 2.8* tells the computer to add the contents of memory locations 1000 and 1002.

The processor contains four key components (*Fig. 2.9*): a clock, an instruction control unit, an arithmetic and logic unit, and a set of registers. The **clock** generates precisely timed pulses of current that synchronize the processor's other components. The **instruction control unit** determines the location of the next instruction to be executed and **fetches** it from main memory. The **arithmetic and logic unit** executes that instruction. It consists of the circuits that add, subtract, multiply, divide, compare, copy, and initiate input or output — the computer's **instruction set**. **Registers** are temporary storage devices that hold control information, key data, and intermediate results.

Machine Cycles

Exactly how do a computer's internal components work together to execute an instruction? Let's use a model of a simple computer system (*Fig. 2.10a*) to illustrate a few **machine cycles**. Begin with the processor. In addition to the clock (not shown in this figure), it contains an instruction control unit, an arithmetic and logic unit, and several registers, including an instruction counter, an instruction register, and a work register called the accumulator. The computer's other major component, main memory, holds program instructions and data values. The numbers preceding the instructions and data values are main memory addresses.

The process starts when the clock generates a pulse of current, which activates the instruction control unit. Its job is to decide what the machine will do next. The computer is controlled by program instructions, and the instructions, remember, are stored in main memory. The address of the next instruction to be executed is found in the instruction counter (*Fig. 2.10a*). The instruction control unit checks the instruction counter, finds the address, and fetches the next instruction, placing it in the instruction register (*Fig. 2.10b*). Fetching an instruction from memory takes time, giving the instruction control unit an opportunity to increment the instruction counter to point to the next instruction (*Fig. 2.10b*, again).

At a precise interval, the clock generates another pulse of current. This one activates the arithmetic and logic unit, which executes the instruction stored in the instruction register (*Fig. 2.10c*). Note that, following execution of the instruction, a data value is copied from main memory to the accumulator register.

Fig. 2.10   A computer executes one instruction during each machine cycle.

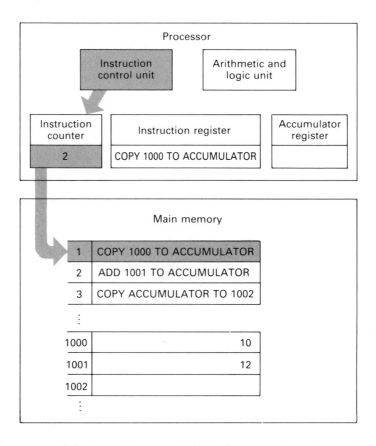

a.   As our example begins, main memory holds both program instructions and data. The instruction register points to the first instruction to be executed.

Fig. 2.10

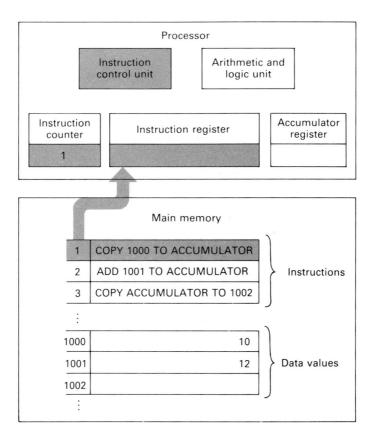

b. In response to a fetch command from the instruction control unit, the first instruction is copied from memory and stored in the instruction register. Note that the instruction counter points to the *next* instruction.

Fig. 2.10

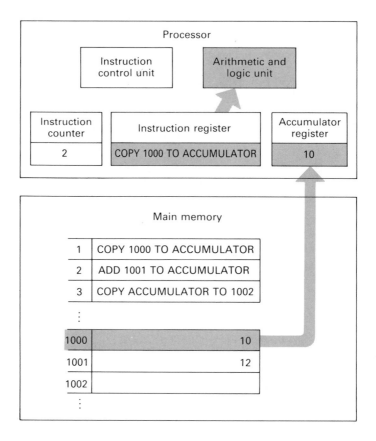

c. Next, the arithmetic and logic unit gets control, and executes the instruction in the instruction register. Thus, a data value is copied from main memory and loaded into the accumulator register.

Once again, the clock ticks. Thus, it's back to the instruction control unit, where the next machine cycle begins (*Fig. 2.10d*). Referring to the instruction counter, the instruction control unit fetches the next instruction and copies it into the instruction register (*Fig. 2.10e*). Once again, note that the instruction register now points to the next instruction.

Fig. 2.10

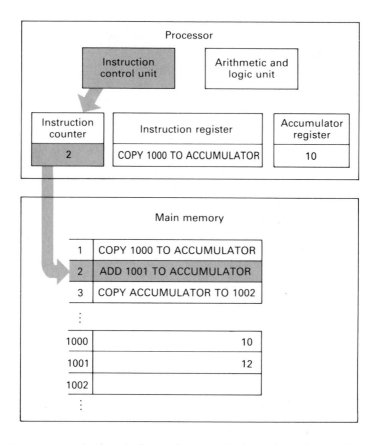

d. As the next cycle begins, the instruction control unit regains control and looks to the instruction register for the address of the next instruction.

Fig. 2.10

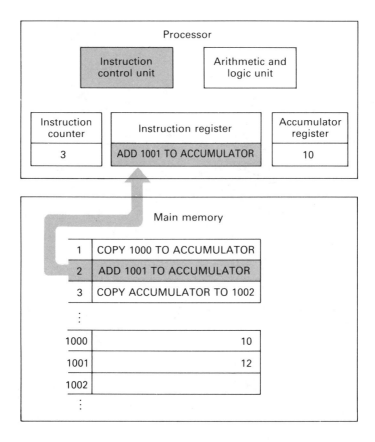

e. The next instruction is fetched and copied into the instruction register. Note that the instruction counter points to the *next* instruction.

The clock ticks. The arithmetic and logic unit gets control and executes the instruction in the instruction register (*Fig. 2.10f*); thus a data value from memory is added to the accumulator.

Fig. 2.10

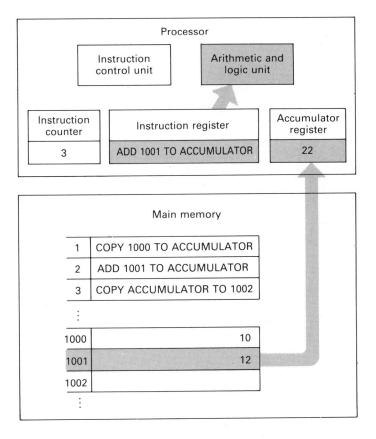

f.   The arithmetic and logic unit executes the instruction in the instruction register. Two values are added, and their sum is placed in the accumulator register.

The next clock pulse takes us back to the instruction control unit. As before, the instruction counter points to the next instruction (*Fig. 2.10g*), and this instruction is fetched and copied into the instruction register (*Fig. 2.10h*). As before, the next clock pulse gives control to the arithmetic and logic unit, which executes the instruction (*Fig. 2.10i*), storing the sum in main memory.

Fig. 2.10

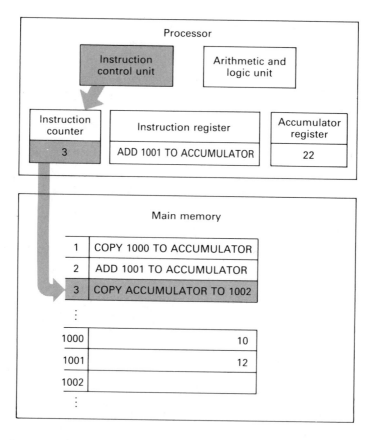

g. As the next cycle begins, the instruction control unit looks to the instruction counter for the address of the next instruction.

Fig. 2.10

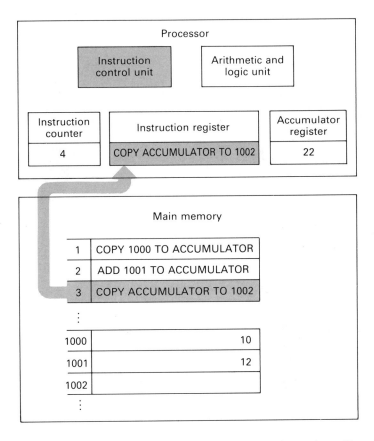

h. The next instruction is fetched and copied into the instruction register. Note that the instruction counter points to the *next* instruction.

Fig. 2.10

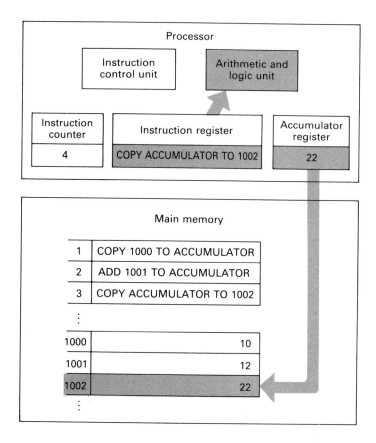

i.   The arithmetic and logic unit executes the instruction in the instruction register. The result is stored back in main memory.

Fig. 2.11 The basic machine cycle is repeated over and over again, until all the instructions in the program have been executed.

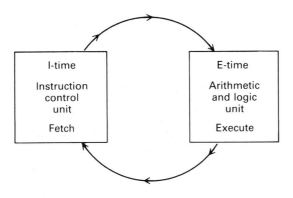

An instruction is fetched by the instruction control unit during **I-time**, or **instruction time**, and executed by the arithmetic and logic unit during **E-time** or **execution time** (*Fig. 2.11*). This process is repeated over and over again until the program is finished. The clock drives the process, generating pulses of current at precisely timed intervals. The rate at which these clock pulses are generated is what determines the computer's operating speed. On many modern computers, clock time is measured in nanoseconds (billionths of a second), so the machine can exceute millions of instructions per second!

Summary

At this point, we know a computer is a machine that processes data (stored in main memory) into information, under control of a stored program. We also know that, internally, a computer is a binary machine; thus the data and the program instructions must be stored in binary form. Characters are represented in a binary code. Numbers are stored as binary numbers, with each bit's positional value significant. A computer's main memory is divided into bytes, words or both (depending on the system), and each of these basic storage units is assigned an address. Using this address, the processor can read or write selected bytes or words.

The processor consists of a clock, an instruction control unit, an arithmetic and logic unit, and registers. Once a program is stored in main memory, the processor can begin to execute it. During I-time, the instruction control unit fetches an instruction from main memory; during E-time, the arithmetic and logic unit executes it. Precisely timed electronic pulses generated by the clock drive this basic machine cycle.

What is the source of the data? How does a program get into main memory? These questions will be answered in the next two chapters.

Key Words

- address
- arithmetic and logic unit
- binary
- bit
- byte
- central processing unit (CPU)
- clock
- execution time (E-time)

- fetch
- instruction
- instruction control unit
- instruction set
- instruction time (I-time)
- integrated circuit memory
- machine cycle
- main memory

- main processor
- operand
- operation code
- processor
- RAM (random access memory)
- register
- ROM (read-only memory)
- word

Self Test

1. Positional values in the binary number system are factors of
   _____ .

   a. ten
   b. two

   c. eight
   d. sixteen

2. A physical switch is _____ ; its setting is _____ .

   a. software/hardware
   b. hardware/software

   c. hardware/data
   d. data/information

3. A _____ holds enough bits to store a single character.

   a. word
   b. byte

   c. bit
   d. chip

4. A _____ is a group of _____ .

   a. bit/bytes
   b. byte/words

   c. word/bytes
   d. character/bytes

5. Inside a computer, characters are represented by _____ .

   a. a binary code
   b. words

   c. registers
   d. positional values

6. The "digit-times-place-value" rule works with _____ , but not with _____ .

a. numbers/characters
b. bits/bytes

c. bytes/words
d. characters/numbers

7. A location in memory is accessed by its _____ .

a. address
b. value

c. content
d. register

8. When memory is _____ , its contents are not changed.

a. written
b. accessed

c. read
d. it's always changed

9. When memory is _____ , its contents are changed.

a. written
b. accessed

c. read
d. it's always changed

10. The programmer can read and write _____ .

a. ROM
b. RAM

c. words
d. bytes

11. What type of memory can only be read?

a. registers
b. ROM

c. RAM
d. words

12. The processor fetches and executes _____ .

a. clock pulses
b. data

c. instructions
d. information

13. The part of an instruction that tells the processor what to do is the

_____ .

a. operand
b. pulse

c. statement
d. operation code

14. What part of an instruction identifies the memory locations that are to participate in the operation?

a. operation code
b. pulse

c. statement
d. operand(s)

15. The processor's components are synchronized by _____ .

    a. instructions   c. information
    b. data   d. clock pulses

16. Which processor component fetches the next instruction from main memory?

    a. instruction counter   c. instruction control unit
    b. instruction register   d. arithmetic and logic unit

17. Which processor component executes instructions?

    a. instruction register   c. arithmetic and logic unit
    b. instruction control unit   d. main memory

18. Which processor component holds key control information such as the address of the next instruction to be executed?

    a. registers   c. instruction control unit
    b. main memory   d. arithmetic and logic unit

19. An instruction is fetched during _____ .

    a. I-time   c. cycle time
    b. E-time   d. run time

20. An instruction is executed during _____ .

    a. E-time   c. run time
    b. cycle time   d. I-time

21. One instruction is fetched and executed during a single _____ .

    a. clock pulse   c. memory access
    b. instruction   d. machine cycle

Answers

1.b 2.b 3.b 4.c 5.a 6.a 7.a 8.c 9.a 10.b 11.b 12.c 13.d 14.d
15.d 16.c 17.c 18.a 19.a 20.a 21.d

Relating the Concepts

1. Inside a computer, data are stored and manipulated in binary form. Why binary?

2. How do bits, bytes, and words differ?

3. How is a computer's main memory addressed?

4. Distinguish between a memory location's address and its contents.

5. Distinguish between ROM and RAM.

6. What is an instruction?

7. What happens during a single machine cycle? Relate the machine cycle concept to the computer's internal components; in other words, explain how these components work together to execute instructions.

8. What are registers? What are registers used for?

9. In Chapter 1, Exercise 5, you were asked to sketch the components of a typical computer system. In this chapter, you have studied the processor and main memory in more detail. Add that detail to your sketch.

3.

Input and Output

KEY CONCEPTS

Accessing a computer

Basic I/O
- Keyboards and display screens
- Printers

Graphics
- Graphic output
- Graphic input

Other input and output devices
- Punched cards
- Printers
- Magnetic media
- Optical media
- Terminals
- Voice recognition/ voice response

Linking the components
- Interfaces
- Channels and control units

Accessing a Computer

A computer is a machine that processes data into information. Unless some human being needs the information, there is no point to processing the data. Without data, there are nothing to process. Input and output devices provide a means for people to access a computer. In this chapter, we'll consider a number of input and output devices and media, and then show how they are physically linked to a computer.

Basic I/O

Keyboards and Display Screens

The basic input device on most small computer systems is a **keyboard** (*Fig. 3.1*). As characters are typed, they are stored in main memory (*Fig. 3.2a*), and then copied from memory to the basic output device, a **display screen** (*Fig. 3.2b*). In effect, the screen (*Fig. 3.3*), often called a **monitor**, serves as a window on main memory, allowing the user to view its contents.

Fig. 3.1 The basic input device on most small computer systems is a keyboard.

Fig. 3.2. Input and output.

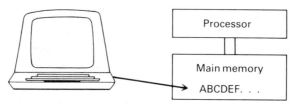

Processor

Main memory

ABCDEF. . .

a. As characters are typed, they are stored in the computer's main memory.

Fig. 3.2

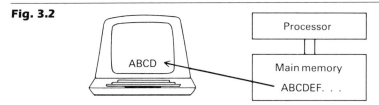

b. Selected characters are then output from main memory to the display screen.

Fig. 3.3 The basic output device on most small computer systems is a display screen.

Several different types of displays are available. Some show white characters against a black background; options include green and amber screens. Color monitors display characters, charts, pictures, and diagrams in color. Standard television sets are sometimes used as inexpensive display devices, but, because the clarity of a television signal suffers when small elements (such as letters and digits) are displayed, real computer monitors produce a much sharper image.

Printers

The image displayed on a screen is temporary; it fades as soon as the power is cut. By routing the output to a **printer** (*Fig. 3.4*), a permanent copy (called a hard copy) is obtained. Dot matrix printers form characters from patterns of dots; they are inexpensive, but the output can be difficult to read. Letter-quality printers type complete, solid characters, and produce a clean, sharp impression. More exotic techniques form images by spraying ink or by selectively burning (carbonizing) the surface of the paper.

Fig. 3.4   A printer generates more permanent hard-copy output.

Graphics

Graphic Output

Computers are not limited to displaying characters; **graphic** output (*Fig. 3.5*) is possible, too. Remember that a computer's output comes from main memory. Thus, if a graphic image is to be displayed, it must first be constructed in memory. Memory stores bits. How can a cartoon character, a bar chart, or a schematic drawing be defined as a pattern of bits?

Fig. 3.5   Increasingly, computers are being used to generate graphic output as well as character output.

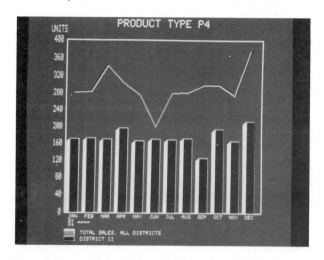

Poloroid

The secret is to divide the screen into a grid of picture elements, or **pixels** (*Fig. 3.6*). Each pixel represents a dot or a point; by selectively turning the points on or off, a picture is formed. The on/off state of each pixel is, essentially, binary, and can be stored in memory. As memory is scanned, the picture elements are displayed, and the image appears.

The quality, or **resolution**, of the picture is a function of the number of pixels. For example, a single, large picture element can show no detail; the screen is either all black or all white. With nine pixels (a 3 x 3 grid), it is possible to form a single, rough character, much as light bulbs form characters on a scoreboard. As the number of picture elements increases, finer and finer details can be displayed. Of course, there is a cost for this improvement; since information about each pixel must be stored, high-resolution graphics requires more memory than low-resolution graphics.

Graphic output displayed on a screen is temporary. For a hard copy, the image can be sent to a plotter (*Fig. 3.7*).

Fig. 3.6   To display graphic output, the screen is divided into a grid of picture elements, or pixels. Each pixel represents one point. Pictures are formed by turning selected pixels on and off.

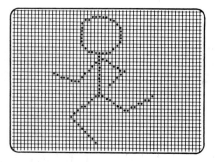

Fig. 3.7   A plotter generates permanent hard-copy graphic output.

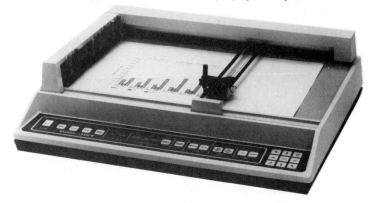

Bausch & Lomb Instruments and Systems Division

Graphic Input

How might a person manipulate or interact with a picture once it is displayed? One way to generate graphic input is by controlling the **cursor**. Usually seen as a blinking line or a box, the cursor indicates the position where the next character typed will appear.

Perhaps the best-known device for controlling the cursor is a joystick (*Fig. 3.8*); if you have ever played a computer game, you have probably used one. Similar cursor control can be obtained with a mouse (*Fig. 3.9*), a small, palm-sized device with a roller on the bottom. The mouse is placed on a flat surface. Move it forward, and the cursor moves up; move it to the left, and the cursor moves to the left, and so on. Like a joystick, a mouse moves the cursor relative to its present position. The cursor control keys found on many keyboards perform the same function.

The cursor's position defines a point on the screen. Pushing a button on a joystick or a mouse or pressing the enter key inputs the cursor's current position. Given the cursor's position, the stored program can take appropriate action. With a touch screen (*Fig. 3.10*) or a light pen (*Fig. 3.11*), a user enters a point simply by touching a spot on the screen.

Fig. 3.8   Perhaps the best-known device for controlling the cursor is a joystick.

Measurement Systems, Norwalk, Connecticut

Fig. 3.9   The cursor's position can also be controlled by manipulating a mouse, or by pressing the keyboard's cursor control keys.

Cortron, A Division of Illionois Tool Works, Inc.

Fig. 3.10 A mouse or a joystick can also be used to input the x-y coordinates of selected points. An option is to use a touch screen.

Carroll Touch Technology

Fig. 3.11 A light pen or stylus can also be used to enter selected points.

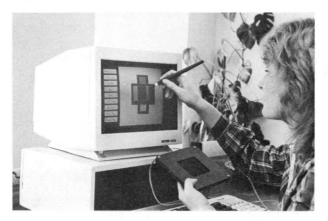

Sun-Flex Touchpen

A digitizer (*Fig. 3.12*) is used to input graphic data. The source document (an engineering drawing, for example) is placed on a tablet, and a reference (often, the lower left corner or the center) is established. Next, the digitizer is moved to a significant point such as the juncture of two lines, a button is pushed, and the point's x-y coordinates are transmitted into the computer. The user enters all the key points by moving the digitizer methodically over the source document. Later, a plotter can reproduce the drawing by connecting the points.

Fig. 3.12 Graphic data can be input to a computer with a digitizer. The idea is to enter key points relative to a fixed reference point. Later, a plotter can reproduce the drawing by connecting the points.

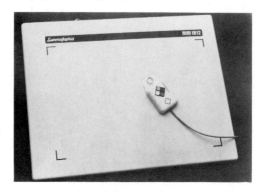

Summagraphics Corporation

Other Input and Output Devices

Punched Cards

Punched cards (*Fig. 3.13*) were among the very first computer input media. The standard card is composed of eighty columns, each divided into twelve rows. As characters are typed through a keypunch, they are recorded as patterns of holes in a column; for each possible row/column position, there either is or is not a hole. A card reader converts the hole patterns to electronic form. Note the similarity between a card's hole/no hole patterns and binary.

Fig. 3.13 The punched card was one of the first computer input media.

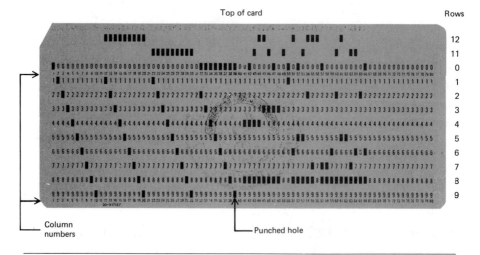

Printers

Most microcomputer printers print one character at a time, usually at rates varying from 30 to perhaps 180 characters per second. The speed is fine for a few pages of output. Imagine, however, printing a 200-page accounting report at 100 characters per second. Assuming a 120-character line and 50 lines per page, the report would take over three hours to print! A more reasonable approach is to use a line printer (*Fig. 3.14*) which, as the name implies, prints line by line instead of character by character. Rates of 1000 lines per minute (and more) are common; at 1000 lines per minute, the accounting report described above could be printed in ten minutes. Even greater speed can be obtained by using a page printer to churn out complete pages at a time. For more compact output or long-term storage, computer output microfilm (COM) can be used.

Fig. 3.14   A line printer prints a complete line at one time.

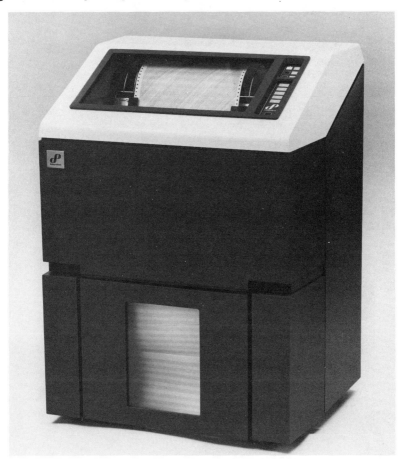

Magnetic Media

Several common input media rely on **magnetic** properties. For example, the characters on the bottom of most checks (*Fig. 3.15*) are printed with a special magnetic ink called MICR (magnetic ink character recognition), and can be read electronically. Another banking medium is the magnetic stripe card (*Fig. 3.16*). The strip of magnetic tape holds such data as a customer's account number and credit limit, and is read much like sound recording tape.

Fig. 3.15   Most bank checks are imprinted using a special magnetic ink called MICR.

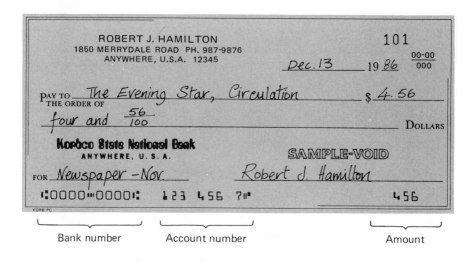

Bank number   Account number   Amount

Fig. 3.16   A magnetic stripe card.

Optical Media

Other media are read **optically**. For example, consider standardized test forms (*Fig. 3.17*). Students use a black pencil to mark their answers. The white paper reflects light; the black spots reflect much less; variations in the intensity of the reflected light can be converted to an electronic pattern. OCR (optical character recognition) equipment uses the same principle to read typed or even handwritten material. Bar codes, such as the Universal Product Code (UPC) printed on most supermarket packages, can be read at a checkout station (*Fig. 3.18*) or by a variety of hand-held scanners (*Fig. 3.19*).

Fig. 3.17 A test score sheet is read optically.

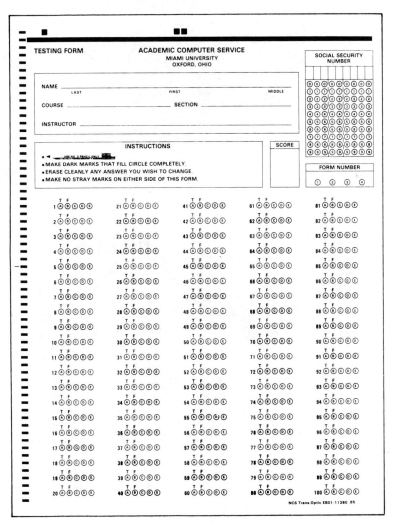

Fig. 3.18 Supermarket checkout stations contain built-in scanners to read the universal product code printed on most packages.

National Semiconductor DATACHECKER/DTS

Fig. 3.19 Hand-held scanners can also read the universal product code. They are often used by sales personnel to collect inventory and sales data.

Interface Mechanisms, Inc.

Terminals

Terminals (*Fig. 3.20*) are also popular. Often, a hundred or more are linked to a single central computer by communication lines. A "dumb" terminal is simply a keyboard and a display screen. An intelligent terminal contains its own memory and processor and can perform many data processing functions on its own. Other special-purpose terminals are designed for a specific function. Examples include automatic bank teller terminals (*Fig. 3.21*), and the supermarket checkout stations described earlier.

Fig. 3.20 A terminal is a keyboard/display unit linked to a central computer via some type of communication line.

TeleVideo Systems, Inc.

Fig. 3.21 An automatic teller machine is a good example of a special-purpose terminal.

NCR Corporation

Fig. 3.22   For certain limited applications, voice recognition equipment is already available.

Interstate Electronics Corporation

Voice Recognition/Voice Response

Perhaps the most natural way of communicating with a computer is by **voice**. Voice response (output) is already used in such mundane applications as children's toys and video games. Due to the tremendous variety of human speech patterns, voice recognition (input) is much more difficult, but significant advances have been made. For certain limited applications, voice recognition is already here (*Fig. 3.22*).

Linking the Components

Interfaces

We know that data are stored in a computer as patterns of bits. Within a given machine, the patterns are consistent; for example, if the code for the letter A is 01000001, this pattern, and *only* this pattern, will be used to represent an A inside the computer.

The rule does not apply to input or output devices, however. On a keyboard, each key generates one character. With graphics, pixels are displayed. A dot matrix printer represents characters as patterns of dots. A card reader interprets patterns of holes punched in a card. An optical device reads light intensity, while a magnetic device reads magnetic intensity. Each input or output device represents or interprets data in its own unique way, and the signals used by a peripheral device may or may not match the signals stored inside the computer. If these dissimilar devices are to communicate, translation is necessary. This is the function of the **interface** board.

Consider, for example, a keyboard. When a key is pressed, an electronic signal is sent to the keyboard's interface. In response, the interface generates the code used to represent that character inside the computer, and transfers the coded data into main memory (*Fig. 3.23a*). Let's change the device to a printer (*Fig. 3.23b*). As output begins, the data are stored inside the computer as binary-coded characters. The printer requires a dot pattern. Clearly translation is necessary. The coded characters are sent to the printer's interface, which translates the computer's binary codes to printer form.

The printer and the keyboard are different; the signals that physically control them and the electronic patterns they use to represent data are device-dependent. However, because the device-dependent tasks are assigned to the respective interface boards, both can be attached to the same computer. On input, an interface board translates external signals into a form acceptable to the computer. Output signals are electronically converted from the computer's internal code to a form acceptable to the peripheral device. Because they are electronically different, a printer and a keyboard require different interface boards. In fact, every input or output device needs a unique interface board to translate its device-dependent signals to (or from) the computer's internal code.

Fig. 3.23   The functions of an interface board.

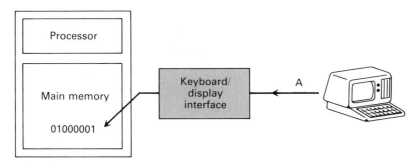

a.   Input from the keyboard enters the interface and is converted to the computer's internal form.

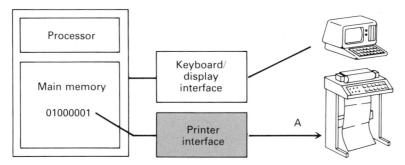

b.   Data stored in main memory are sent to the printer interface, converted to printer form, and output.

Many interface boards contain **buffers**. A buffer is temporary memory or storage used to adjust for the speed differential between two devices. For example, if you've ever waited for a lengthy paper to print, you are almost certainly aware that the printer is much slower than the computer. If waiting for the printer is a problem, you can add a buffer to your printer interface. Then, instead of having the computer send the contents of main memory directly to the printer, it can send the information to the buffer at computer speed. A short time later, as the characters are dumped from the buffer to the printer at printer speed, you can use the computer for some other task.

Channels and Control Units

The use of one interface board per device is reasonable on a microcomputer system. However, on a large system with hundreds of peripheral devices, this approach is simply unworkable. Instead, input and output devices are linked to a large computer system through **channels** and **control units**.

Certain functions (for example, deciding where the next byte can be found or stored in memory and counting the characters transferred to or from an external device) are common to almost all types of input and output. On a microcomputer, they are performed by each interface board; in effect, they are duplicated for each device on the system. On larger machines, these common functions are assigned to data channels (*Fig. 3.24*).

Note that a channel handles device-*independent* functions. What about such device-*dependent* functions as interpreting magnetic patterns? They are implemented through I/O control units or interface units (*Fig. 3.24*). Each physical device has its own control unit. The channel communicates with the computer in the computer's language; the control unit communicates with the external device on the device's terms; the channel and the control unit, working together, translate.

A typical large computer system may have three or four channels, with numerous control units attached to each one. This is a very flexible approach. It allows hundreds of input and output devices to access the computer over only a few easy to control data paths.

Fig. 3.24   On a large computer system, peripheral devices are linked to the system through a channel and an I/O control unit.

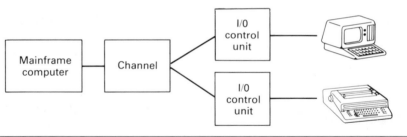

Summary

Human beings access a computer through its input and output devices. The basic input device on most small computer systems is the keyboard. As a user types characters, they are stored in the computer's main memory. From there, they are output to a display screen (the basic output device), where the user can see them.

If a permanent copy of the output is required, it can be sent from memory to a printer. Computers are not limited to character output, however; many systems support graphics. A screen is divided into a number of points called pixels. Images are formed by selectively turning the pixels on and off. A screen's resolution is a function of the number of pixels. We briefly considered several other input and output devices and media, including punched cards, various types of printers, magnetic media, optical media, terminals, and voice I/O.

Finally, we turned to the problem of linking input and output devices to a computer system. Each device is electronically different, but the computer always deals with a common code. An interface board serves to bridge this gap. An input device sends its data to the interface, which converts the data from the external device's form to the computer's internal form and stores them in main memory. On output, information moves from memory to the interface, where it is converted to the external device's form, and output. A buffer can help to adjust for the speed differential between adjacent devices. On larger computers, each external device is linked to a control unit. The control units are plugged into channels, and the channels are connected to the computer.

In this chapter, we have focused on input and output, showing how human beings communicate with a computer. One of the advantages of putting data into a computer is that, once they have been converted to electronic form, they can be used over and over again. In the next chapter, we'll consider long-term secondary storage.

Key Words

- buffer
- channel
- control unit, I/O
- cursor
- display screen
- graphics
- interface
- keyboard
- magnetic media
- monitor
- optical media
- pixel
- printer
- punched card
- resolution
- terminal
- voice I/O

Self-Test

1. The basic input device on a small computer is a _____ .

   a. display screen   c. keyboard
   b. printer   d. card reader

2. The basic output device on a small computer is a _____ .

   a. keyboard   c. diskette
   b. display screen   d. plotter

3. A _____ generates hard-copy output.

   a. display unit   c. monitor
   b. screen   d. printer

4. A display screen is divided into a grid of _____ .

   a. bytes   c. pixels
   b. bits   d. words

5. The _____ indicates where on the screen the next character will appear.

   a. pixel   c. cursor
   b. picture element   d. x-y coordinate

6. On a _____ , data are recorded as patterns of holes.

   a. dot matrix printer c. digitizer
   b. punched card   d. all of the above

7. The characters on the bottom of a check are read _____ .

   a. optically   c. magnetically
   b. by contact   d. they aren't read

8. Standardized test forms are read _____ .

   a. magnetically   c. optically
   b. by physical contact d. by terminals

9. Often, a hundred or more _____ are linked to a single centralized computer by communication lines.

a. OCR devices   c. scanners
b. terminals   d. printers

10. External devices are linked to a small computer system through
_____ .

a. channels   c. plugs
b. control units   d. interfaces

11. The _____ translates between the computer's internal codes
and a peripheral device's external codes.

a. processor   c. memory
b. interface   d. register

12. A(n) _____ is temporary storage used to allow for the speed
disparity between adjacent devices.

a. buffer   c. control unit
b. interface   d. channel

13. On a large computer system, a _____ links external devices to
the computer, and also performs a number of device-independent tasks.

a. channel   c. buffer
b. control unit   d. register

14. On a large computer system, a _____ links external devices to
a channel.

a. control unit   c. register
b. buffer   d. the link is direct

Answers

1.c 2.b 3.d 4.c 5.c 6.b 7.c 8.c 9.b 10.d 11.b 12.a 13.a 14.a

Relating the Concepts

1. What is the function of a computer's input and output devices?

2. List several input devices. List several output devices. How can you tell
which is which? Don't just cite the book. Think about your answer.

3. What is a pixel? Relate pixels to a screen's resolution.

4. What is a cursor? List several devices for controlling the cursor's position.

5. Briefly explain how magnetic media work.

6. Briefly explain how optical media work.

7. What is an interface? Why are interfaces necessary?

8. What is a buffer? Why are buffers necessary?

9. What is a channel? What is an I/O control unit? Distinguish between the functions performed by a channel and the functions performed by an I/O control unit.

10. On microcomputers, peripheral devices are linked to the system through interface boards. On a large mainframe, peripherals are linked through I/O control units and channels. Why?

4.

Secondary Storage

KEY CONCEPTS

Why secondary storage?

Secondary storage media
- Magnetic cassette
- Diskette
- Hard disk
- Other secondary storage media

Accessing secondary storage

Why Secondary Storage?

One advantage of a computer is that once data have been entered, they can be stored on the machine and accessed repeatedly. Generating address labels for a magazine is a good example. Instead of retyping all the labels for each edition, subscriber data are input once, stored, and then dumped from storage whenever necessary. Programs provide another example. Like the subscriber data, they are stored on the computer and accessed on demand.

Where exactly are the data and the programs stored? The obvious answer is main memory, but main memory is expensive, and the supply on most machines is limited. Another problem is its volatility; main memory loses its contents when the power is cut. We need a fast, accurate, inexpensive, high-capacity, nonvolatile extension of main memory, and **secondary storage** fills this need.

Secondary Storage Media

Magnetic Cassette

The least expensive of the secondary storage media is magnetic **cassette**, the same cassette tape used to record music. Data are output to a tape recorder. By playing the "recording" back, the material is restored to main memory. Cassettes are inexpensive and compact, but they are also relatively slow and error prone. They are used on some small home computer systems or for archival storage.

Diskette

The most common microcomputer secondary storage medium is **diskette** or **floppy disk** (*Fig. 4.1*), a thin circular piece of flexible polyester coated with a magnetic material. Data are recorded on one or both flat surfaces. Because contact with dust, lint, or even a human finger can destroy the data, each diskette has its own protective jacket. A diskette drive works much like a record turntable. The round hole in the center of the **disk** allows the drive mechanism to engage and spin it; an **access mechanism**, analogous to the tone arm, reads and writes the surface through the window visible near the bottom of Fig. 4.1.

The data are recorded on a series of concentric circles called **tracks** (*Fig. 4.2*). The access mechanism steps from track to track, reading or writing one at a time. The tracks are subdivided into **sectors**; it is the contents of a sector that move between the diskette and main memory. To distinguish the sectors, they are addressed by numbering them sequentially—0, 1, 2, and so on.

When a program instruction requesting diskette input is encountered, the processor sends a control signal to the drive. In response, the drive spindle is engaged, and the disk begins to spin, quickly reaching a constant rotational speed (*Fig. 4.3a*). Next, the access mechanism is moved to the track containing the desired data (*Fig. 4.3b*). The time required to bring the drive up to speed and position the access mechanism is called **seek time**. Remember that data are transferred between the diskette and main memory a sector at a time. The desired sector may be anywhere on the track. The time required for the sector to rotate to the access mechanism (*Fig. 4.3c*) is called **rotational delay**.

Fig. 4.1   The most popular microcomputer secondary storage medium is diskette.

3M

Fig. 4.2   Data are recorded on a series of concentric circles called tracks. The tracks, in turn, are subdivided into sectors. Data move between the disk surface and main memory a sector at a time.

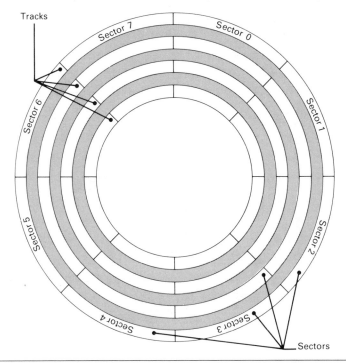

Fig. 4.3   Reading a sector from disk.

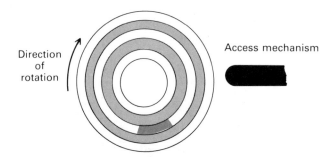

a.   First, the disk drive is brought up to operating speed.

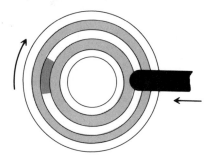

b.   Next, the access mechanism is positioned over the track that holds the desired data. The time required to perform steps a and b is called seek time.

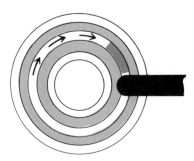

c.   Finally, the system must wait until the desired sector rotates to the read/write head (rotational delay) before the data are transferred into main memory.

Although diskette is certainly faster than cassette, data access still means a delay of at least a fraction of a second. Many common personal computer applications involve only limited disk access, so the delay is hardly noticeable. On other applications, however, the delay can be intolerable. The solution is often a **hard disk**.

Hard Disk

A diskette drive spins only when data are being read or written. The drive must be brought up to operating speed before the read/write heads can be moved and the data accessed, and that takes time. A hard disk (*Fig. 4.4*), in contrast, spins constantly. Since it is not necessary to wait for the drive to reach operating speed before moving the access mechanism, seek time is significantly reduced, often to a few thousandths of a second. Further improvements are gained by spinning the disk more rapidly (1000 revolutions per minute or more), which reduces rotational delay. Data stored on hard disk can be accessed far more rapidly than data stored on diskette.

Another advantage of hard disk is its storage capacity. A typical double-sided diskette might hold 360,000 characters. A hard disk for a microcomputer system might store 20 to 30 *million* characters.

With slow diskette drives, the access mechanism rides directly on the disk surface. At 1000 revolutions per minute, however, any physical contact between the disk surface and the read/write head would quickly destroy both; thus, a hard disk's access mechanism rides on a cushion of air, a few millionths of an inch above the surface (*Fig. 4.5*). (Shaped like an airfoil, the read/write head literally flies.) Because such pollutants as a smoke particle, dust, or a human hair won't fit between the head and the surface, a hard disk is normally encased in an airtight container to protect it from the environment.

Fig. 4.4   Unlike diskette, a hard disk rotates constantly. As a result, seek time is reduced. Because of a hard disk's high rotational speed, rotational delay is reduced, too.

Quantum

Fig. 4.5   A hard disk's access mechanism rides on a cushion of air a few millionths of an inch above the disk surface.

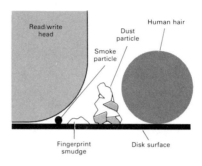

Although single-surface disks do exist, particularly on small systems, most large computers use **disk packs** consisting of several recording surfaces stacked on a common drive shaft (*Fig. 4.6*). Typically, each surface has its own read/write head. The heads are arrayed on a single, comblike access mechanism. All the heads move together. Imagine, for example, that the access mechanism is positioned over track 30. The top read/write head will access track 30 on surface 0. Moving down, surface by surface, the second head will be over track 30 on surface 1, the third over track 30 on surface 2, and so on. One position of the access mechanism corresponds to one track on each surface. This set of tracks is called a **cylinder**.

Fig. 4.6   On a disk pack, each surface has its own read/write head. The heads are arrayed on a single, comb-like access mechanism. Thus they all move together.

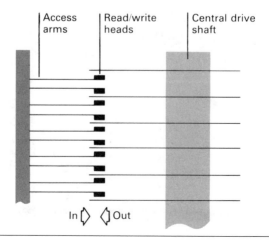

Fig. 4.7   Some disk packs are fixed; others, however, can be changed. Here, an operator is removing a disk pack from a drive. Subsequently, a new pack will be mounted on the same drive, thus making more data available to the computer.

Accessing disk begins with seek time. The access mechanism is moved to a selected cylinder, and a selected head is activated. The system is now looking at a single track. Next, the desired data rotate to the read/write head—rotational delay. Finally, the data are read and transferred into the computer.

A disk pack, such as the one shown in Fig. 4.7, is mounted on a disk drive containing a spindle and an access mechanism. Packs can be changed. If a disk pack is dismounted, a different pack's data can be accessed through the same set of read/write heads. With the newer Winchester technology, the pack and the access mechanism are sealed together in an airtight container, giving each pack its own set of heads. Winchester disks are popular on smaller computer systems.

Given the tremendous capacity of a disk pack, losing one, through human error, fire, flood, or similar disaster, can destroy a great deal of important data. In most large computer centers, the data are regularly backed up by copying them. Should a disk pack be lost, the **backup** copy is used to restore the data.

Other Secondary Storage Media

Magnetic tape (*Fig. 4.8*) is one of the most common backup media. Tape is fast, with data transfer rates comparable to disk. Its storage capacity is quite high, and a reel of tape is relatively inexpensive. Unfortunately, data can be read or written only in a fixed sequence, which limits tape to a few application areas.

Fig. 4.8 Magnetic tape is one of the most common backup media.

Kennedy Company, Monrovia, California

The original secondary storage device was **magnetic drum** (*Fig. 4.9*). As the name implies, a drum is a cylinder coated on the outside surface with the same magnetic material that coats disk and tape. Data are stored on parallel tracks that encircle the surface. Each track has its own read/write head. Since no head movement is required, there is no seek time—magnetic drum is very fast. However, compared to disk, drum has limited storage capacity and is quite expensive.

One of the newest secondary storage media is **video disk**. These disks are read and written by a laser beam; there is no physical contact between the recording surface and the read/write mechanism. Fast, accurate, compact, and easy to use, video disk has a promising future.

Fig. 4.9 The first secondary storage device was the magnetic drum.

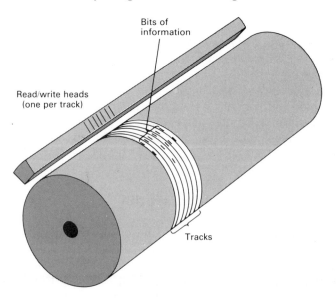

Accessing Secondary Storage

On a small computer, secondary storage devices are linked to the system through interface boards (*Fig. 4.10*). The interface board physically controls the disk drive, accepting seek, read, and write commands from the processor, positioning the access mechanism, and controlling the flow of data between the disk surface and main memory. On a large computer, channels and I/O control units are used (*Fig. 4.11*). The channel communicates with the computer. The control unit communicates with the external device.

Because of its storage capacity, a single disk can hold hundreds of programs, or the data for dozens of different applications. If you are a computer user, however, you want a particular program, and you want to access a particular set of data. How does the computer find the right program or the right data?

Fig. 4.10   On a small computer, secondary storage devices are linked to the system through interface boards.

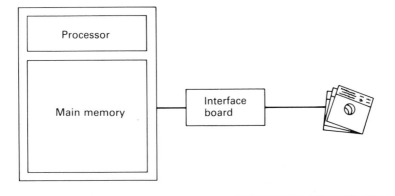

Fig. 4.11   On a large computer, a secondary storage device is linked to the computer through a channel and an I/O control unit.

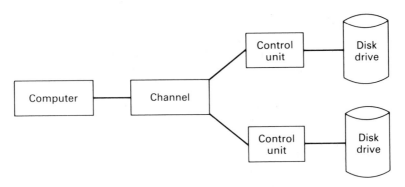

Start by reviewing how data are stored on disk. The surface is divided into tracks, which, in turn, are divided into sectors. Data are stored in the sectors as patterns of bits. The tracks are numbered sequentially. The outer track is 0. As we move toward the center of the disk, the next track is 1, then 2, and so on. The sectors are also numbered sequentially. The first sector on a track is 0, the second is 1, then 2, and so on. Track 5, sector 8 is a particular sector; track 5, sector 9 is a different sector; and track 6, sector 8 is yet another one. Each sector on the disk has a unique track/sector address.

When a program is stored on disk, it is normally recorded in a set of *consecutive* sectors. Thus, if the program starts on track 3, sector 0, you can assume that it's continued on track 3, sector 1, and so on. If the computer can find a program's beginning, it can find the entire program.

How does the system determine where a particular program begins on disk? Several sectors on the first track are normally set aside to hold an **index** or **directory** (*Fig. 4.12*). When the program is first written to disk, it is assigned a name, which is recorded in the index, along with the track and sector address where the program begins. Later, to retrieve the program, a user enters the program's name. The computer then reads the index, searches it for the name, finds the address where the program begins, and reads the program.

Fig. 4.12   An index is maintained to keep track of the programs and data files stored on a disk.

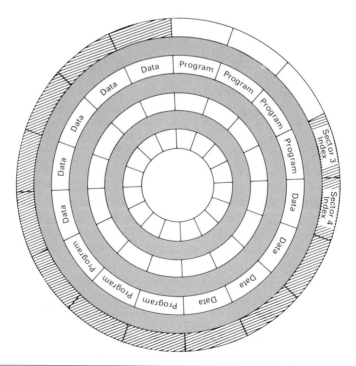

Data are accessed in much the same way. The data for a given application are grouped to form a file; we'll talk more about data files in Chapter 8. Each file is assigned a name. The file name and the address of its first sector are recorded in the disk's index. Because the data that make up a file are normally stored in consecutive sectors, knowing the first sector's address allows the system to find the others.

Secondary storage is an *extension* of main memory, not a replacement for it. A computer cannot execute a program stored on disk unless it is first copied into main memory. A computer cannot manipulate the data stored on a secondary medium until they have been copied into main memory. Main memory holds the current program and the current data; secondary storage is long-term storage.

The input and output devices described in Chapter 3 provide human access to the computer system. Secondary storage does not. Data are stored in a form convenient to the computer, and can be read and written only by the machine. The only way people can access the data stored on a disk is by instructing the computer to read them into main memory and then output them to a display screen or a printer.

Summary

The chapter began with a brief discussion of the need for secondary storage. Because of its cost, limited capacity, and volatility, main memory cannot be used for long-term or for volume storage. Secondary storage is a solution.

Magnetic cassette is the least expensive of the secondary storage media. The most popular microcomputer medium is diskette. Data are stored on the disk's surface on a series of concentric circles called tracks. The tracks are subdivided into sectors. On input, the contents of one sector are copied from disk to main memory; on output, one sector moves from memory to the disk's surface. To access disk, it is first necessary to bring the drive up to operating speed and then move the access mechanism over the track containing the desired data (seek time). Additional time is lost waiting for the desired sector to rotate to the read/write head (rotational delay).

Unlike diskette, a hard disk spins constantly; thus a major component of seek time is eliminated. Because hard disk rotates faster than diskette, it has less rotational delay. Hard disk has more storage capacity than diskette, too. On diskette, the read/write head normally rides directly on the disk surface. With hard disk, the access mechanism rides a few millionths of an inch above the surface on a cushion of air. Often, several surfaces are stacked on a single drive shaft to form a disk pack. A disk pack normally has one read/write head per surface, with the heads grouped on a single access mechanism. One position of the access mechanism thus defines one track on each surface; this group of tracks is called a cylinder.

Because data can be so valuable, disk packs are normally backed up. Magnetic tape is a common backup medium. The first secondary storage medium was magnetic drum. Video disk shows promise for the future.

On a small system, secondary storage devices are linked to the computer through interface boards. On larger systems, an I/O control unit physically controls the disk drive, while a channel communicates with the computer.

A single disk can contain numerous programs and data files. To distinguish them, an index is maintained. The index identifies the programs and data files and indicates the track and sector address where each one begins. Given the address of the first sector, the other sectors can be located.

Secondary storage is an extension of main memory. The computer cannot execute a program until it has been loaded into main memory, nor can it process data until they have been copied into main memory. Secondary storage cannot be read by human beings; it is a machine-readable medium.

Key Words

- access mechanism
- backup
- cassette
- cylinder
- directory
- disk
- disk pack

- diskette
- floppy disk
- hard disk
- index
- magnetic drum
- magnetic tape
- rotational delay

- secondary storage
- sector
- seek time
- track
- video disk

Self-Test

1. Which of the following is not a problem with main memory?

   a. volatility
   b. limited capacity
   c. cost
   d. speed

2. The most common microcomputer secondary storage medium is
   _____ .

   a. diskette
   b. hard disk
   c. magnetic tape
   d. video disk

3. Data on disk are recorded on a series of concentric circles called
   _____ .

   a. sectors
   b. cylinders
   c. blocks
   d. tracks

4. Data are transferred between main memory and the disk surface a
   _____ at a time.

a. track   c. sector
b. cylinder   d. word

5. The time delay during which the disk drive is brought up to operating
    speed and the access mechanism positioned is _____ .

    a. access time   c. seek time
    b. rotational delay   d. I-time

6. The time during which the desired sector rotates to the access mecha-
    nism is called _____ .

    a. rotational delay   c. run time
    b. access time   d. seek time

7. A _____ rotates constantly.

    a. diskette drive   c. hard disk
    b. cassette drive   d. floppy disk drive

8. On hard disk, rotational delay is less than on diskette because rotational
    speed is _____ .

    a. eliminated   c. increased
    b. it isn't   d. decreased

9. Several disks stacked on a single drive spindle form a _____ .

    a. cylinder   c. disk pack
    b. drum   d. video disk

10. On a disk pack, one position of the access mechanism accesses a set of
    tracks called a _____ .

    a. word   c. block
    b. sector   d. cylinder

11. A common backup medium is _____ .

    a. diskette   c. magnetic drum
    b. magnetic tape   d. video disk

12. On a *small* computer, secondary storage devices are linked to the system
    through _____ .

    a. control units   c. interface boards
    b. channels   d. software

13. On a *large* computer system, which communicates with the disk drive?

    a. channel   c. I/O control unit
    b. interface board   d. processor

14. The combination of a sector number and a track number forms a unique
    _____ .

    a. index   c. disk address
    b. program name   d. file name

15. The address of the beginning of each program stored on a disk is found in
    the disk's _____ .

    a. program   c. index
    b. controller   d. interface

Answers

1.d 2.a 3.d 4.c 5.c 6.a 7.c 8.c 9.c 10.d 11.b 12.c 13.c 14.c
15.c

Relating the Concepts

1. Why is secondary storage necessary?

2. Imagine a set of data stored in main memory. Explain the process of
   transferring the data to disk. Be specific; explain each step in the process.

3. What is the difference between a diskette and a hard disk? What advantages are gained by using hard disk?

4. What is a disk pack?

5. Distinguish between a cylinder, a track, and a sector.

6. What is backup? Why is backup necessary?

7. How are secondary storage devices physically linked to a computer? How
   are input and output devices linked to a computer? Compare your answers.

8. Explain how a computer finds the "right" data or the "right" program
   stored on disk.

9. Secondary storage is an extension of main memory. Explain.

10. In Chapter 1 (Exercise 5) you sketched a simple computer system. In Chapter 2 (Exercise 9) you added more detail to that sketch. In Chapters 3 and 4, you learned how input, output, and secondary storage devices are linked to a system. Once again, modify your sketch, showing how the peripherals are physically linked. You might want to prepare two sketches—one for a microcomputer and one for a mainframe.

5.

Linking
the Components

Micros and Mainframes

Up to this point, we have studied a computer's primary components one by one. You know that a computer contains a processor, main memory, and several registers, and that numerous input, output, and secondary storage devices can be attached, but you probably tend to view those components as independent boxes. It's time to link the pieces. In this chapter, we'll investigate a number of ways a computer's components can be assembled.

Bus Lines and Cables

A computer is a system. Data flow between its components in response to instructions executed by the processor. Sometimes, the bits are transmitted in **parallel**; other components communicate in **serial**. Picture a one-lane bridge with automobiles crossing in single file. Now, picture a four-lane bridge with traffic in each lane. Clearly, the four-lane bridge can move more traffic in a given amount of time. The same general rule holds for serial and parallel lines. A parallel line consists of several wires and thus can transmit several bits at a time. A serial line consists of a single wire, so only one bit can be transmitted at a time. Parallel lines are faster.

Bus lines, such as the ribbon-like set of parallel wires pictured in Fig. 5.1, link the computer's internal components and are used to attach secondary storage devices to the system. They transmit data in parallel. Input and output devices are connected to the system by cables. Parallel cables consist of several wires; serial cables consist of a single wire and are used to attach slower peripherals.

Fig. 5.1　A computer's internal components are linked by ribbon-like bus lines. External devices are attached to the system by cables.

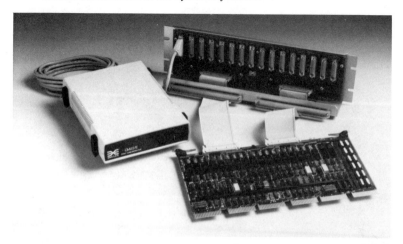

Word Size

Communication between the components is greatly simplified if they are electronically similar. Thus, on most systems, the processor, main memory, buses, interfaces, and channels are all designed around a common **word** size. For example, on a 32-bit computer, the processor manipulates 32-bit numbers, main memory and the registers store 32-bit words, and data and instructions move between the components over 32-bit bus lines. Almost any word size will do, although 4, 8, 16, and 32 bits are the most common.

A computer's word size affects its processing speed, memory capacity, precision, and cost. Let's consider speed first. A 32-bit bus contains 32 wires, and thus can carry 32 bits at a time. A 16-bit bus has only 16 parallel wires, and thus can carry only 16. Because the wider bus moves twice as much data in the same amount of time, the 32-bit machine is clearly faster. Generally, the bigger the word size, the faster the computer.

Memory capacity is also a function of word size. To access main memory, the processor must transmit over a bus the address of a desired instruction or data element. On a 32-bit machine, a 32-bit address can be transmitted. The biggest 32-bit number is roughly 4 billion in decimal terms; thus the processor can access as many as 4 billion different memory locations. On the other hand, a 16-bit computer transmits a 16-bit address, limiting it to roughly 64,000 memory locations. Generally, the bigger its word size, the more main memory a computer can access.

There are 16-bit microcomputers that access considerably more than 64K bytes of memory. How is that possible? A 16-bit machine can access more than 64K if addresses are broken into two or more parts and transmitted during successive machine cycles. Each cycle takes time, however, so memory capacity is gained at the expense of processing speed.

Next, consider the size of the numbers each machine can manipulate. A 16-bit computer works with 16-bit numbers; a 32-bit machine works with 32-bit numbers. More digits mean more precise answers. Many 16-bit computers can transfer and work with 32-bit numbers, but need two cycles to fetch the number from memory, and two more to manipulate it. On a smaller machine, precision, like memory capacity, is achieved at the expense of processing speed.

Low-cost, 4-bit microprocessors are used in a variety of consumer products, including automobiles, household appliances, and even children's toys. Many inexpensive **microcomputers** are designed around an 8-bit word; this small word size limits their memory capacity, processing speed, and precision (*Fig. 5.2*). More expensive micros and most **minicomputers** use a 16-bit word, giving them greater speed, more main memory, and greater precision. **Mainframes** are typically constructed around a 32-bit word, and, consequently, are even bigger, even faster, and even more precise. Some expensive scientific "supercomputers" have a 60- or 64-bit word.

Word size also influences a system's cost. Most 8-bit machines are priced well under $1000, while more powerful 16-bit micros sell for $2,000 or more (*Fig. 5.2*). A typical minicomputer costs about $10,000, while a mainframe might sell for $100,000, and a maxi can easily exceed $1 million. There is a great deal of overlap, with inexpensive 16-bit "minis" competing with surprisingly powerful 32-bit "supermicros," and "superminis" performing traditional mainframe tasks. The terms micro, mini, and mainframe are guidelines, not absolutes.

Discussing such factors as word size, bus width, speed, memory capacity, precision, and cost makes it easy to overlook the obvious. Microcomputers (*Fig. 5.3*) are small and have a limited number of peripherals. Mainframes (*Fig. 5.4*), on the other hand, are much larger and typically support a vast array of input, output, and secondary storage devices.

Fig. 5.2 A comparison of computer types.

Computer type	Word size	Cycle time	Memory capacity	Cost	Examples
Home microcomputer	8 bits	microseconds	64K bytes	about $1000	Apple IIc, Apple IIe
Professional microcomputer	16 bits	a microsecond	256K bytes	over $2000	IBM PC
Minicomputer	16 bits	250 nanoseconds	512K bytes	$10,000 +	DEC PDP-11
Mainframe	32 bits	50 nanoseconds	4 megabytes	$100,000 +	IBM 3083, 4361
Supercomputer	64 bits	10 nanoseconds	4 + megabytes	$1 million +	Cray X-MP/2

Fig. 5.3 A typical microcomputer system.

AT&T Bell Laboratories

Fig. 5.4   A mainframe computer system.

International Business Machines Corporation

Microcomputer Architecture

If we were to remove the cover from a microcomputer and a mainframe, we'd see that, although both contain similar components, those components are assembled in different ways. Computer scientists use the term **architecture** when discussing the relationships among a computer system's components. Let's investigate.

Microcomputers are sold to individuals, often to computer novices. Applications are generally small, with brief programs processing limited amounts of data. While few microcomputer users match this profile exactly, it is a reasonable generalization. A computer designed to sell in such a market will stress low cost, ease of use, and reliability, while sacrificing, if necessary, processing speed, precision, memory capacity, and peripheral devices. Keep these factors in mind as we examine the architecture of a microcomputer system.

Most systems are constructed around a **motherboard** (*Fig. 5.5*), a metal framework containing a series of **slots** linked, through a bus, to an 8- or 16-bit processor (*Fig. 5.6*). Memory is added by plugging a memory board into one of the open slots (*Fig. 5.7*). Without input and output, the computer is useless, so a keyboard/display interface, is plugged into another slot, and a keyboard and display unit connected to it (*Fig. 5.8*). A printer can be attached through a printer interface, and if a diskette interface is plugged into an open slot, a diskette drive can be added. We now have a complete microcomputer system.

Fig. 5.5 A microcomputer is constructed around a metal framework called a mother-board. Typically, the processor and related components are mounted on the motherboard, and a bus links the processor to a series of slots that are used to attach other boards to the system.

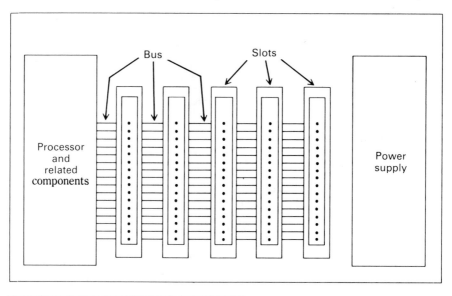

Fig. 5.6 A schemetic drawing showing a processor and a motherboard. A bus links the processor with a number of slots into which components can be plugged.

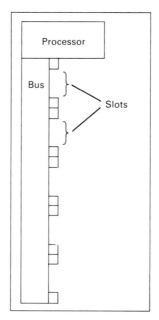

Fig. 5.7 A memory board is plugged into one of the open slots.

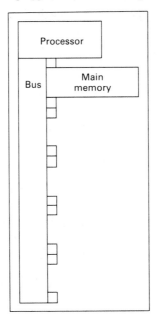

Fig. 5.8 Input devices, output devices, and secondary storage devices are added to the system by plugging the appropriate interface into an open slot and then running a cable from the external device to the interface.

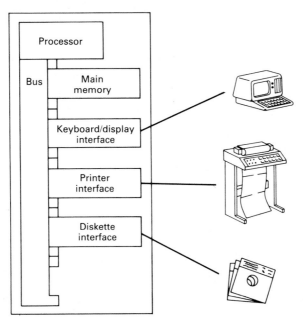

There is one more open slot available on our hypothetical system. We could use it to add more main memory, or another disk drive, or another printer, or some other peripheral device, but we can't add them all because the number of available slots limits the expandability of a microcomputer system. Remember, however, the nature of a typical microcomputer user. Most require only limited capacity; thus, the fact that the architecture limits expandability is not a serious problem. Perhaps those who desire more capacity really need a mini or a mainframe.

The components pictured in Fig. 5.8 are linked by a common bus. This arrangement is called **single-bus architecture** (*Fig. 5.9*). All communications between components flow over this bus, under the control of the processor.

Fig. 5.9   A typical microcomputer uses a single-bus architecture, with all internal components linked by a single bus line.

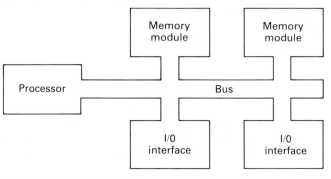

Fig. 5.10   The process of loading and executing a program involves several steps.

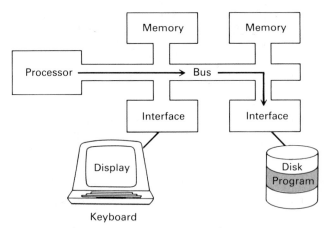

a.   In response to a user's request to run a program, the processor sends a signal over the bus to the disk interface.

For example, consider loading and executing a program. First, in response to a user's command, a signal is sent over the bus to the disk interface (*Fig. 5.10a*). Responding to the signal, the disk interface communicates with the disk drive, which reads the program and transfers it over the bus and into main memory (*Fig. 5.10b*). Once the program is in memory, the processor can execute it by fetching its instructions one by one (*Fig. 5.10c*). Of course, the instructions move from memory to the processor over the bus. Finally, as the program's instructions are executed, input data move from a peripheral device, over the bus, and into main memory (*Fig. 5.10d*), while output moves from memory, over the bus, and to an output device.

Fig. 5.10

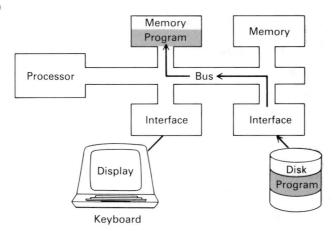

b. The program is transferred from the disk surface, through the interface, across the bus, and into main memory.

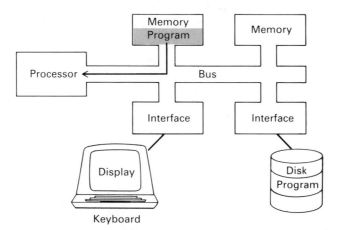

c. Once the program is in memory, the processor can execute it, fetching its instructions, one by one, over the bus.

Fig. 5.10

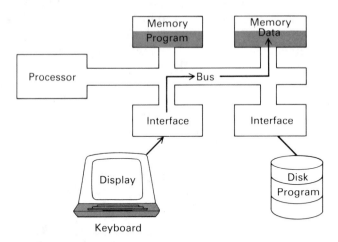

d. As the program is executed, input data move from an input device, through an interface, across the bus, and into main memory.

Because the electronic signals controlling a keyboard/display unit, a printer, and a diskette drive are different, each peripheral device has its own interface. One side communicates with the computer, using internal codes (*Fig. 5.11*). The other side is device-dependent, communicating with the external device in its own terms. The basic function of the interface is translation. For example, the letter A is represented physically both as a key on a keyboard and as a dot pattern on a printer. When a user types A, an electronic pulse enters the keyboard/display interface where it is translated to the binary code that represents an A inside the computer. Later, on output, this same code is sent to a printer interface, where it is translated to the electronic signals needed to form the proper dot pattern. Note that the computer always uses the same binary code, no matter what peripheral device is involved. To the processor all peripheral devices look alike.

Fig. 5.11   The basic function of an interface is to translate between internal and external data forms.

Mainframe Architecture

Because a microcomputer is designed for a single user, single-bus architecture is reasonable. A mainframe, however, is designed for a different mix of applications. Often, the system is the repository for the organization's key operating and planning data. The idea is to have all users access this common, central data base. With numerous users and vast amounts of data, both primary and secondary storage capacity are crucial. Also, numerous input and output devices will be needed. Programs are typically large and complex, so processing speed is important, too.

A system with a 32-bit processor, a million or more bytes of main memory, scores of secondary storage devices, and numerous input and output devices is quite expensive, so efficiency is a key management concern. Forcing an expensive computer to wait while a human being types a line of input is absurd. The solution is to design the system to execute several programs concurrently, with the processor switching its attention to program B while data are being input for program A. We'll examine concurrent processing in more detail in Chapter 10. Meanwhile, let's consider its impact on a mainframe's architecture.

Controlling input and output involves such logical functions as selecting the path over which the data are to flow, counting characters, and computing main memory addresses. The processor is the only source of logic on a microcomputer system; thus the processor must be directly involved in each I/O operation. While it is controlling I/O, the processor is not available to execute application program instructions, but given the nature of a microcomputer system, this is a minor problem.

However, on a big computer supporting multiple users, it makes sense to execute several programs concurrently. A mainframe's basic machine cycle is identical to a microcomputer's—its processor still fetches and executes one instruction at a time. How can such a machine execute two or more programs concurrently? The key is freeing the processor from responsibility for input and output. Most large systems assign the task of controlling I/O to channels (*Fig. 5.12*). A channel is a micro- or minicomputer with its own processor; it can perform logical functions in parallel with the computer's main processor, thus freeing the main processor to do other things.

Fig. 5.12 On a mainframe, device-independent functions are assigned to a channel, and device-dependent functions are assigned to an I/O control unit.

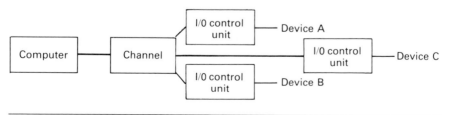

Some I/O functions are device-dependent; for example, controlling the movement of an access arm is a disk problem, while converting characters to a dot pattern is unique to a dot matrix printer. Other tasks, such as selecting a data path, counting characters, and computing main memory addresses, are common to all input and output operations, no matter what peripheral device is involved. The channel handles these device-independent functions, while the device-dependent functions are assigned to an I/O control unit (*Fig. 5.12*). Each physical device has its own control unit.

A channel moves data between main memory and a peripheral device. The computer's processor manipulates data in main memory. Allowing a channel and a processor to access memory simultaneously won't work on a microcomputer system, because the single-bus architecture of a micro provides only one physical data path. Simultaneous operation requires independent data paths, so most mainframes use **multiple-bus architecture** (*Fig. 5.13*).

Fig. 5.13 Many mainframes use multiple-bus architecture.

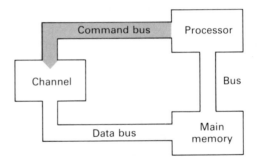

a. The main processor starts an I/O operation by sending a signal to the channel.

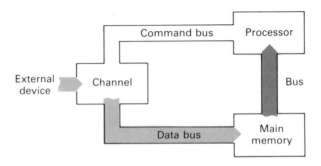

b. The channel assumes responsibility for the I/O operation, and the processor turns its attention to another program.

Fig. 5.13

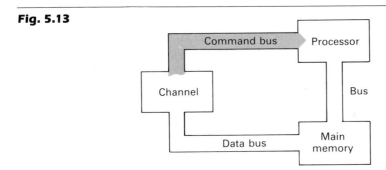

c. The channel sends an interrupt to the processor to signal the end of the I/O operation.

Let's examine how an input or output operation might be supported on a multiple-bus machine. The main processor starts an I/O operation by sending an electronic signal over the command bus to the channel (*Fig. 5.13a*). As program A's data move into main memory over the channel's data bus (*Fig. 5.13b*), the processor, using its own data bus, might be manipulating program B's data. When the I/O operation is finished, the channel notifies the processor by sending an electronic signal called an **interrupt** over the command bus (*Fig. 5.13c*). The processor can now return to program A.

Physically, a mainframe is similar to a microcomputer. Start with a much larger motherboard consisting of a number of slots linked by bus lines. Circuit boards holding key internal components are plugged into the slots. On a micro, each peripheral device has its own interface board. On a mainframe, channels replace the interfaces (*Fig. 5.14*), and several external devices are attached to each one. Instead of a single bus linking all components, most mainframes have multiple bus lines providing independent paths between the components (*Fig. 5.14*); this allows for the simultaneous operation of the processor and the channels, which, in turn, allows the system to support multiple concurrent users.

Fig. 5.14 A mainframe computer might have several channels, with numerous control units and peripheral devices attached to each one.

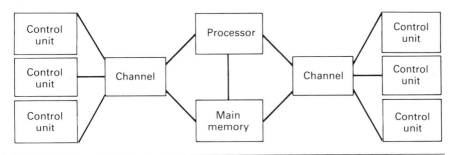

Once again, when we focus on electronics, we tend to overlook the obvious. A mainframe might support dozens of secondary storage devices and hundreds of input and output devices. If the one-slot-per-device rule were still in effect, the mainframe would have to be huge just to provide space for plugging in all those peripherals. Instead, only a few channels are directly linked to the computer. In turn, peripheral devices are plugged into the channels. This flexible design allows the same basic mainframe to support a small system or a large, multiple-channel system with hundreds of peripherals.

Summary

In the first four chapters, we considered a computer's major components. In this chapter, we turned our attention to assembling them. A computer's internal components are linked by bus lines. Peripheral devices are linked by cables. Bus lines and parallel cables move data in parallel, several bits at a time. Serial cables move data bit by bit.

On most computers, the internal components are designed around a common word size. The choice of a word size affects a computer's speed, memory capacity, precision, and cost. Sometimes, memory capacity and precision can be increased by sacrificing processing speed.

A microcomputer is constructed around a metal framework called a motherboard. Features are added by plugging memory boards and various interface boards into available slots; the number of slots limits the number of peripherals that can be added. Typically, each peripheral device requires its own interface board.

Mainframes often support multiple concurrent users. Rather than wasting the main processor's time controlling input and output, the responsibility for I/O is transferred to a channel, which communicates with the computer, handling a number of device-independent functions. Those tasks depending on the external device are assigned to control units, which are plugged into the channels. Because a channel contains its own processor, it can work simultaneously with the main processor. When a channel completes an I/O operation, it notifies the main processor by sending it an electronic signal called an interrupt.

Key Words

- architecture
- bus
- interrupt
- mainframe
- microcomputer
- minicomputer
- motherboard
- multiple-bus architecture
- parallel
- serial
- single-bus architecture
- slot
- word

Self Test

1. A computer's internal components are linked by _____ .

   a. cables
   b. software

   c. bus lines
   d. they aren't

2. Data flow over a bus in _____ .

   a. serial
   b. parallel

   c. either
   d. neither

3. On a _____ line, the bits are transmitted one by one.

   a. parallel
   b. concurrent

   c. serial
   d. sequential

4. On most computers, all the internal components are designed around a common _____ .

   a. bus
   b. machine cycle

   c. word size
   d. clock cycle

5. Word size affects a computer's _____ .

   a. speed
   b. memory capacity

   c. precision
   d. all of the above

6. On a microcomputer system, _____ can be sacrificed for memory capacity.

   a. processing speed
   b. word size

   c. precision
   d. all of the above

7. Most microcomputers are constructed around a metal framework called a _____ .

   a. mainframe
   b. motherboard

   c. slot
   d. bus

8. The number of peripherals that can be linked to a microcomputer is limited by the number of available _____ .

   a. slots
   b. bus lines

   c. channels
   d. all of the above

9. Most microcomputers use _____ architecture.

   a. multiple-bus   c. concurrent
   b. single-bus   d. standard

10. On a microcomputer system, each peripheral device has its own
    _____ .

    a. channel   c. control unit
    b. interface   d. bus line

11. On a *microcomputer*, the _____ directly controls I/O.

    a. channel   c. bus
    b. processor   d. interface board

12. On a *large* computer, the _____ controls I/O.

    a. channel   c. control unit
    b. main processor   d. interface board

13. On a large computer, functions that are unique to a given peripheral de-
    vice are assigned to a(n) _____ .

    a. control unit   c. channel
    b. interface board   d. processor

14. Most mainframes use _____ architecture.

    a. single-bus   c. concurrent
    b. multiple-bus   d. overlapped

15. A channel notifies the processor that an I/O operation is complete by
    sending an electronic signal called a(n) _____ .

    a. pulse   c. interrupt
    b. command   d. they don't communicate

Answers

1.c 2.b 3.c 4.c 5.d 6.a 7.b 8.a 9.b 10.b 11.b 12.a 13.a 14.b
15.c

Relating the Concepts

1. Distinguish between parallel and serial data transmission.

2. How are a computer's internal components physically linked?

3. On most computers, all internal components are designed around a common word size. Why?

4. Explain how a computer's word size affects its processing speed, main memory capacity, and precision.

5. Distinguish between a microcomputer, a minicomputer, and a mainframe.

6. In describing a microcomputer's architecture, we used the terms motherboard, slot, and bus. Relate these terms.

7. What does the term architecture mean when it is applied to a computer?

8. On a typical microcomputer system, each input, output, and secondary storage device has its own interface. Why?

9. Distinguish between single-bus architecture and multiple-bus architecture.

10. Briefly, what is an interrupt? You don't yet have enough information to fully define the term, but what do you think an interrupt is? We'll return to this concept in Chapter 10.

6.

The Operating System

KEY CONCEPTS

The hardware/software interface

Communicating with the
operating system
- The command language

The input/output control system

Loading the operating system
- The boot

Some operating systems

The Hardware/Software Interface

The first five chapters focused on a computer's hardware. It's time we turned our attention to software.

When you think of software, you probably think of **application programs**. They support end-user functions, allowing people to perform such tasks as playing a game, writing a paper, laying out a spreadsheet, or generating paychecks. Another type of software, called **system software**, performs its assigned tasks behind the scenes. An excellent example is the **operating system** found on most computers. An operating system serves as an interface (*Fig. 6.1*), bridging the gap between hardware and application software. Thus, as we move from hardware to software, it's appropriate that we consider the operating system first.

What exactly does an operating system do? Basically, it performs a number of support functions. For example, picture an application program stored on disk. Before the program can be executed, it must first be copied into main memory, because the program that controls a computer must be in main memory. The process of copying a program from disk to memory involves considerable logic. The source of a computer's logic is software. Thus, if the application program is to be loaded, there must be a program in memory to control the loading process. That program is the operating system.

Loading programs is only one of the operating system's many support functions. Basically, it is a collection of software modules that insulate the user from the hardware, thus making the system easier to use. Let's investigate the primary functions of a typical operating system.

Fig. 6.1   The operating system serves as an interface between hardware and application software.

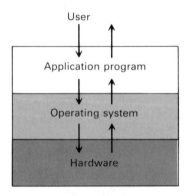

Communicating with the Operating System

Computers are not intelligent. Before the operating system can perform one of its support functions, the person using the computer must tell it what to do. The user, much like a military officer, issues orders. The operating system responds like a sergeant, gathering the necessary resources, and carrying out each command. The operating system module that accepts, interprets, and carries out commands is the **command processor** (*Fig. 6.2*).

The command processor consists of a number of modules, each of which performs a single task (*Fig. 6.3*). For example, one module contains the instructions that guide the computer through the process of copying a program from disk and loading it into main memory. Another contains the instructions that transfer control of the computer to that program.

Fig. 6.2   The operating system module that accepts, interprets, and carries out commands is called the command processor.

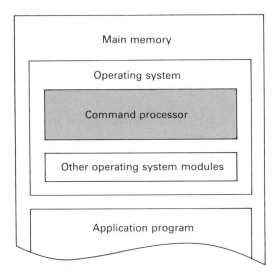

Fig. 6.3   The command processor is composed of a number of program modules, each of which performs a single, logical function.

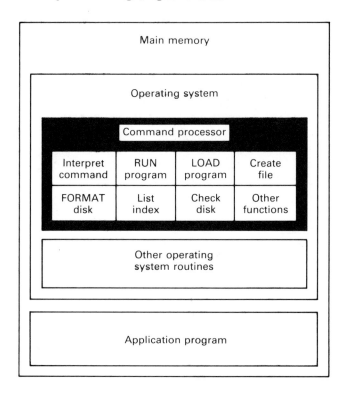

The Command Language

The programmer communicates with the command processor through a **command language**. Generally, there is a simple one-word command for each main function—LOAD (load a program from disk), RUN (execute the program stored in main memory), FORMAT (format a disk), DISKCOPY (copy a disk), and so on. A user sitting at a keyboard types a command. The characters flow from the keyboard, through an interface board, across a bus, and into main memory. Once they're in memory, the command processor interprets the command and gives control to the appropriate functional module.

For example, consider the task of loading and executing a program. As the process begins, a **prompt** (for example), A⟩ is displayed on the screen. In response, the user types

LOAD MYPGM

and presses the enter key (*Fig. 6.4a*). The command flows into main memory. The command processor evaluates it, and, recognizing a LOAD command, transfers control to the program loading module (*Fig. 6.4b*), which reads the requested program from disk into memory. Once the program is loaded, the command processor gets control again, displays another prompt, and waits for the next command (*Fig. 6.4c*).

The next command, we'll assume, is

RUN

It tells the operating system to execute the application program stored in main memory. Following a RUN command, the command processor gives control to the module that starts the application program (*Fig. 6.4d*). When the application program is finished executing, it gives control back to the command processor, which displays a prompt and waits for the next command.

Fig. 6.4 The operating system is responsible for loading an application program and giving it control.

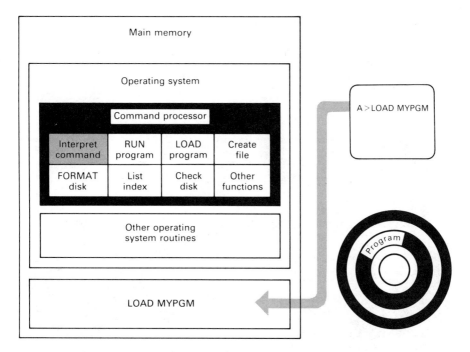

a. Responding to the operating system's prompt, a user types a load command. The command processor then interprets the command.

Fig. 6.4

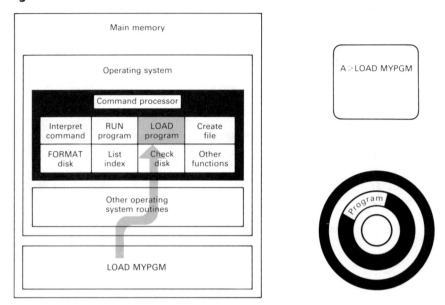

b. The command says to load a program. Thus, the command processor's program loading module gets control.

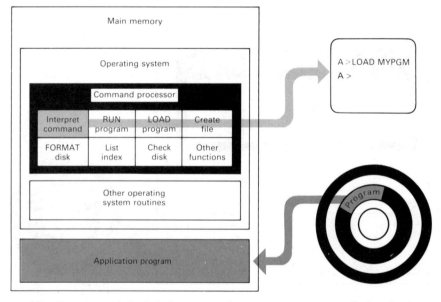

c. After the program is loaded, the command processor gets control, displays it prompt, and waits for the next command.

Fig. 6.4

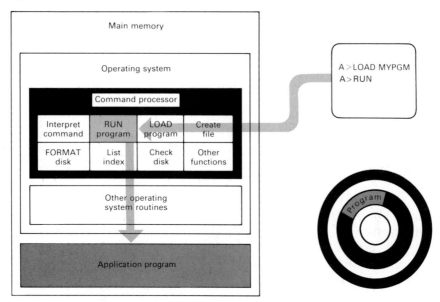

d. The next command tells the operating system to run the program in memory. Thus the command processor gives control to the module that starts the application program.

On most microcomputers, the command processor is the operating system's main control module (*Fig. 6.5*), accepting commands, interpreting them, and determining which lower level modules are needed to carry them out. Those modules communicate directly with the hardware. When they are done, they return control to the command processor, which displays a prompt and waits for the next command. Such systems are said to be command driven.

Fig. 6.5 Most microcomputer operating systems are command driven. A user issues a command. In response, the command processor determines what must be done. After the command has been carried out, the system waits for the next command.

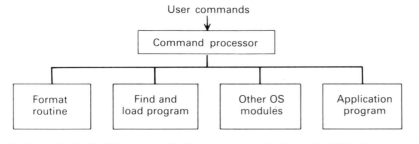

The Input/Output Control System

One of the modules described in the previous section "finds and loads" a program. In explaining it, we glossed over a number of details. There is some logic involved in finding and loading a program.

For example, assume the program is stored on disk. A disk drive contains little or no intelligence; it is limited to performing certain primitive operations, including:

1. Seek to a selected track.
2. Read a selected sector from that track.
3. Write a selected sector to that track.

That's it. That is all a disk drive can do. The only way to read a program from disk into main memory is to send the drive a series of **primitive commands** asking it to seek and read, one by one, each sector that holds part of the program. Note that the disk drive must be told exactly where to position the read/write mechanism, and exactly which sectors to read.

Where do these commands come from? On a computer system, intelligence or logic can come from the human user or from software. Imagine if you had to communicate with the system at a primitive level. If a program were stored on track 20, sectors 8 and 9, you would have to tell the system to:

SEEK 20
READ 8
SEEK 20
READ 9

Of course, it would be your responsibility to remember that the program is stored on track 20, sectors 8 and 9. What if you forgot? Chances are you would never see your program again.

Fig. 6.6   Most operating systems also contain an input-output control system. The IOCS is the module that communicates directly with the peripheral equipment.

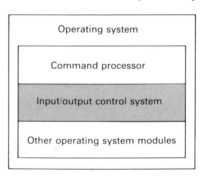

What does the user want? A program. Does he or she really care where that program is physically stored? Probably not. The typical user simply wants the program; the primitive hardware details associated with finding and loading it are (or should be) the computer's concern. This is where the operating system comes into play. Most contain an **input/output control system**, or **IOCS** (*Fig. 6.6*), that generates the necessary primitive commands.

Imagine a program named SPACEWAR is stored on track 20, sector 8. What do you find easier to remember? Track 20, sector 8? Or SPACEWAR? Most people envision programs by name. The objective of an operating system is to insulate the user from the hardware—to make the hardware easier to use. Since people find it easy to remember programs by name, it makes sense to design the input/output control system to accept a name and translate it to physical commands. How is this done?

Remember from Chapter 4 that the various programs stored on a disk are listed in the disk's index (*Fig. 6.7*). This index is the secret to accessing them by name. For example, following the command

LOAD SPACEWAR

the command processor transfers control to the program loading module. That module, in turn, calls on the input/output control system, which reads the index. Once the index is in main memory, the IOCS can search it. Each

---

Fig. 6.7   The index found on each disk is the key to accessing programs by name. Each program on the disk is identified by name, and its location is noted. To load a program, the operating system reads the index, searches it for the desired program's name, extracts the program's location, and then issues the necessary primitive commands to read it.

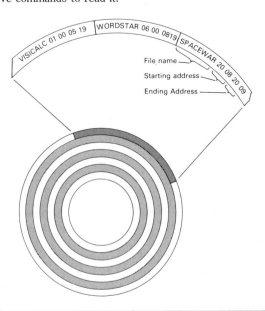

program on the disk is identified by name; note that SPACEWAR is the third entry. Following the program's name is its physical location (in other words, the track and sector holding its first instructions). Using this information, the IOCS issues the necessary seek and read commands, and the program is copied into memory.

That's basically all there is to it. When a program is first written to disk, its name and physical location are recorded in the index. To retrieve the program, the index is read and searched for the name, the program's physical location is extracted from the index, and the necessary primitive I/O commands are issued. The input/output control system manages the index and generates the necessary primitive I/O commands.

Our example was based on accessing disk. The IOCS is responsible for communicating with the system's other peripheral devices, too. Each physical device is controlled by its own unique set of primitive commands. (Incidentally, that's another reason why each input or output device requires its own interface or control unit.) Application programs issue general requests to start input or to start output. The input/output control system accepts these general requests and generates the primitive commands needed to control a specific peripheral device.

However, establishing communication with an external device involves more than just generating primitive commands. For example, whenever two hardware components (such as a computer and a disk drive) communicate with each other, their electronic signals must be carefully synchronized. Synchronization involves exchanging a predetermined set of signals called a **protocol**. Starting or checking protocol signals is a tedious process usually assigned to the operating system.

More generally, a number of details are associated with starting, ending, and controlling any input or output operation. Rather than duplicating the logic to perform these functions in every application program, it makes sense to implement them once, in the operating system's input/output control system, and allow the application programs to access peripheral devices through this module. Once again, we see that the operating system is a hardware/software interface.

Loading the Operating System

Loading and executing a program starts with a command that the operating system reads and interprets. Clearly, the operating system must be in memory before the command is issued. How does it get there? On a few systems, the operating system is stored in read-only memory. ROM is permanent; it keeps its contents even when the power is lost. A ROM-based operating system is *always* there.

However, on most computers, main memory is composed of RAM, or random access memory. RAM is volatile; it loses its contents when the power is cut. Thus, each time the computer is turned on, the operating system must be loaded. Unfortunately, we can't simply type a command, such as LOAD OS, and let the operating system take care of loading itself. Why not? When the computer is first turned on, main memory is empty. If the operating system is not yet in memory, it can't possibly read, interpret, and carry out the command.

The Boot

Typically, the operating system is stored on disk. The idea is to copy it into memory. This objective is achieved by a special program called a **boot** (*Fig. 6.8*). Generally, the boot is stored on the first sector (or two) of a disk. Hardware is designed to read this sector automatically whenever the power is turned on (*Fig. 6.8a*). The boot consists of only a few instructions, but they are sufficient to read the rest of the operating system into memory (*Fig. 6.8b*); note how it is seemingly "pulled in by its own bootstraps." Now, a user can type the commands to load and execute an application program.

Fig. 6.8 The operating system is loaded into main memory by a special program called the boot.

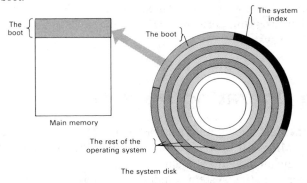

a. When the computer is first turned on, hardware automatically reads the boot program from the first few sectors of a disk.

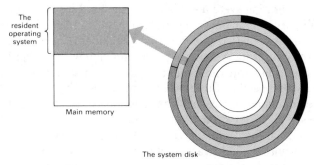

b. The boot routine contains the instructions that read the rest of the operating system from disk into memory.

An Example

Let's use a brief example to summarize what we've learned about the operating system. As we begin, main memory is empty, and a disk containing the boot, the operating system, and an application program has been loaded into the disk drive. As the power is turned on, the boot flows into main memory, and its instructions are executed; as a result, the operating system is copied from disk.

Now, the operating system's command processor module has control of the computer. It displays a prompt and waits for the user to enter a command. The user tells the system to load a program. The command processor reads and interprets the command, and gives control to its program loading module. Since loading a program calls for accessing disk, this module, in turn, calls the input/output control system. The IOCS finds the requested program and copies it into main memory. Control then returns to the command processor, which displays a prompt and waits for the next command.

The next command is RUN. The command processor reads and interprets it and transfers control to the module that starts application programs. The application program gets control, and the user communicates with it. Finally, the application finished, control returns to the command processor, which displays a prompt and waits for the next command. At this point, the user can load another program, perform a system function such as formatting a disk, or signoff the system.

Some Operating Systems

Perhaps the best known microcomputer operating system is **MS/DOS**, developed by Microsoft Corporation for the IBM-PC and compatible machines. It has become an industry standard.

Why is an operating system standard so important? At the hardware level, computers made by different manufacturers are often incompatible; in other words, a program written for one won't work on another. Remember, however, that the operating system sits between the hardware and the application program. With a common operating system in the middle, it is possible for the same program to run on two quite different machines (*Fig. 6.9*). Of course, the portions of the operating system that communicate with the hardware might be very different, but software would see a smooth, common interface.

MS/DOS is composed of three primary modules (*Fig. 6.10*). COMMAND .COM is the command processor. The functions of the input/output control system are divided between two routines, MSDOS.SYS and IO.SYS. MSDOS.SYS is hardware-independent. IO.SYS, on the other hand, communicates directly with the hardware, so it contains device-dependent code. Versions of the operating system written for different computers should differ only in their IO.SYS logic. In addition to the primary modules, the operating system contains a number of utility programs.

Fig. 6.9 The operating system presents the application program with a smooth, consistent interface.

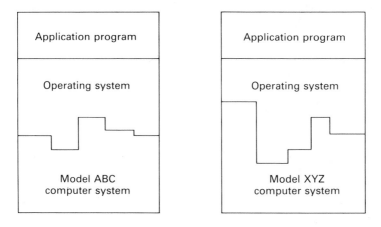

Fig. 6.10 MS/DOS, perhaps the best-known microcomputer operating system, is composed of three primary modules.

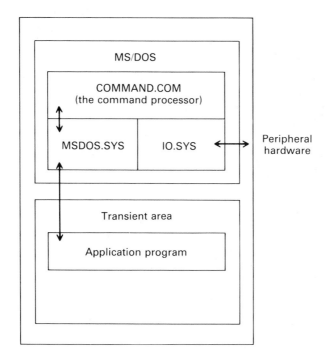

When MS/DOS is booted, COMMAND.COM, MSDOS.SYS, and IO.SYS are copied into main memory. The transient area (*Fig. 6.10*) consists of memory not assigned to the operating system. Application programs, system utilities, certain transient modules, and data are read into the transient area.

Because MS/DOS is so widely used, a vast library of application software has been developed for it. This software library will tend to perpetuate MS/DOS's status as a standard, simply because it makes sense to buy a computer for which software already exists. Virtually every significant microcomputer supplier supports MS/DOS, at least as an option.

Another popular operating system is CP/M, the control program for microcomputers developed for early 8-bit machines by Digital Research, Incorporated. UNIX, developed by American Telephone and Telegraph (AT&T), shows promise of becoming a new standard, particularly for applications involving communication between two or more computers. Mainframes have more complex operating systems which, in addition to serving as a hardware/software interface, manage the computer's resources. We'll consider them in Chapter 10.

Summary

After explaining the difference between application software and system software, we turned to the operating system, a collection of modules serving as a hardware/software interface. Users communicate with the operating system through a command language. The command processor accepts, interprets, and carries out the commands. Most microcomputer operating systems are command driven.

Communicating with input and output devices is difficult because each is controlled by its own primitive commands. The input/output control system (IOCS) accepts generalized requests for I/O and generates the necessary primitives. We used an example to illustrate how the IOCS accepts a program name, searches a disk index, finds the program's location, and reads the program into main memory. Another function of the IOCS is generating and interpreting the protocol signals that are needed to synchronize devices before they begin to communicate.

Because a computer's main memory is volatile, the operating system must be loaded each time the computer is turned on. The routine that loads the operating system is called a boot. Typically stored on the first sector or two of a disk, the boot is read by hardware. Once in memory, it loads the rest of the operating system.

Perhaps the best-known microcomputer operating system is MS/DOS. We briefly considered the components of MS/DOS, relating them to the general functions of an operating system. CP/M is a popular 8-bit operating system. UNIX shows promise of becoming a new standard.

Key Words

- application program
- boot
- command language
- command processor
- input/output control system
- MS/DOS
- operating system
- primitive command
- prompt
- protocol
- system software

Self Test

1. The _____ serves as a hardware/software interface.

   a. system
   b. application program
   c. control unit
   d. operating system

2. The source of a computer's logic is _____ .

   a. hardware
   b. software
   c. data
   d. the user

3. The operating system module that accepts, interprets, and carries out commands is the _____ .

   a. IOCS
   b. command processor
   c. boot
   d. program loader

4. A user communicates with the operating system through _____ .

   a. instructions
   b. a program
   c. hardware
   d. a command language

5. Most microcomputer operating systems are _____ driven.

   a. interrupt
   b. command
   c. software
   d. hardware

6. A disk drive is limited to a few _____ .

   a. tasks
   b. program functions
   c. primitive operations
   d. I/O operations

7. The operating system module that sends a disk drive its primitive commands is the _____ .

   a. command processor   c. boot
   b. IOCS   d. interrupt handler

8. The name and location of each program stored on a disk is found on the disk's _____ .

   a. index   c. interface
   b. label   d. primitive command

9. The _____ is responsible for communicating with all input and output devices.

   a. command processor   c. boot
   b. IOCS   d. system software

10. Before two devices can communicate, they must synchronize by exchanging _____ signals.

    a. boot   c. primitive
    b. interrupt   d. protocol

11. _____ is permanent; _____ is volatile.

    a. Memory/storage   c. ROM/RAM
    b. Storage/memory   d. RAM/ROM

12. The operating system is loaded by _____ .

    a. the command processor   c. the program loader
    b. a boot   d. an interrupt

13. The best-known microcomputer operating system is probably _____ .

    a. MS/DOS   c. VM
    b. MVS   d. CPC

14. _____ shows promise of becoming a new standard, particularly for applications involving communication between two or more computers.

    a. MS/DOS   c. VM
    b. CP/M   d. UNIX

Answers

1.d 2.b 3.b 4.d 5.b 6.c 7.b 8.a 9.b 10.d 11.c 12.b 13.a 14.d

Relating the Concepts

1. Distinguish between application programs and system software.

2. An operating system serves as an interface between application programs and hardware. Explain.

3. An operating system is a collection of software modules, each of which performs a single support function. Explain.

4. What does the operating system's command processor do? Relate the command processor to its command language.

5. What does the operating system's input/output control system do?

6. What are primitive commands? Why are they necessary?

7. Imagine a program named MYPGM that is stored on disk. Briefly explain how the operating system loads it into main memory. Start with the user's command.

8. Explain how an operating system is booted. Why is booting necessary?

9. Sketch the component parts of a microcomputer operating system. Briefly explain what each component does.

10. Sketch the component parts of MS/DOS. Compare its components to the ones in your Exercise 9 sketch.

7.

Application Software

KEY CONCEPTS

What is software?

Programming languages
- Assemblers
- Compilers and interpreters
- Nonprocedural languages

Libraries

The program development process
- Problem definition
- Planning
- Writing the program
- Debug and documentation
- Maintenance

Writing your own program

What Is Software?

In Chapter 6, we learned that an operating system is a collection of software modules that perform support functions, effectively insulating the user from the hardware. In this chapter, we turn to a more general discussion of software. It is *not* our intent to teach you how to program; you're not going to learn by reading a single chapter in an introductory textbook. Instead, we'll try to strip away some of the mystery so often associated with software by showing you, at the machine level, exactly what a program is, and then briefly discussing the process a programmer follows when developing one.

Let's start with a definition. A **program** is a series of **instructions** that guides a computer through a process. Each instruction tells the machine to perform one of its basic functions: add, subtract, multiply, divide, compare, copy, request input, or request output. In Chapter 2, we learned that the processor fetches and executes a single instruction during each machine cycle. A typical instruction (*Fig. 7.1*) contains an operation code that specifies the function to be performed, and a series of operands that specify the memory locations or registers holding the data to be manipulated. For example, the instruction

ADD 3,4

tells a hypothetical computer to add registers 3 and 4.

Fig. 7.1   An instruction is composed of an operation code and one or more operands. The operation code tells the computer what to do. The operand or operands specify the addresses of the data elements to be manipulated.

Operation code	Operands
ADD	3,4

Fig. 7.2   Because a computer's main memory stores bits, the program must exist in binary form. These four instructions are needed to add two numbers on an IBM mainframe computer.

```
0101100000110000110000000000000000

0101100001000000110000000000000100

0001101000110100

0101000000110000110000000000001000
```

Because a computer's instruction set is so limited, even simple logical operations call for several instructions. For example, imagine two data values stored in main memory. To add them on many computers, both values are first loaded (or copied) into registers, the registers are added, and then the answer is stored (or copied) back into main memory. That's four instructions: LOAD, LOAD, ADD, and STORE. If four instructions are needed to add two numbers, imagine the number of instructions in a complete program.

A computer is controlled by a program stored in its own main memory. Because main memory stores bits, the program must exist in binary form. Figure 7.2 shows the binary, machine-level instructions needed to load two numbers into registers, add them, and store the answer in memory.* If programmers had to write in **machine language**, there would be be very few programmers.

Programming Languages

Assemblers

An option is writing instructions in an **assembler** language; for example, Fig. 7.3 shows how two numbers might be added in IBM mainframe assembler. The programmer writes one mnemonic (memory-aiding) instruction for each machine-level instruction. AR (for add registers) is much easier to remember than the equivalent binary operation code: 00011010. L (for load) is much easier to remember than 01011000. The operands use labels, such as A, B, and C, instead of numbers to represent main memory addresses, and that simplifies the code, too.

Fig. 7.3 An assembler program reads a programmer's mnemonic source statements, translates each one to a single machine-level instruction, and then combines them to form an object module.

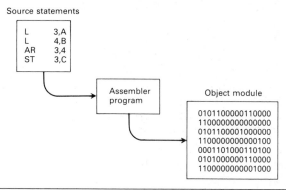

---

* These binary instructions are valid on an IBM 3083 mainframe computer, and on other computers in the IBM System/370 family.

Unfortunately, there are no computers that can directly execute assembler language instructions. Writing mnemonic codes may simplify the programmer's job, but computers are still binary machines and require binary instructions. Thus, translation is necessary. An assembler program (*Fig. 7.3*) reads a programmer's **source code**, translates the source statements to binary, and produces an **object module**. Because the object module is a machine-level version of the programmer's code, it can be loaded into memory and executed.

An assembler language programmer writes one mnemonic instruction for each machine-level instruction. Because of the one-to-one relationship between the language and the machine, assemblers are machine dependent, and a program written for one type of computer won't run on another. On a given machine, assembler language generates the most efficient programs possible, and thus is often used to write operating systems and other system software. However, when it comes to application programs, machine dependency is a high price to pay for efficiency, so application programs are rarely written in assembler.

Compilers and Interpreters

A computer needs four machine-level instructions to add two numbers, because that's the way a computer works. Human beings shouldn't have to think like computers. Why not simply allow the programmer to indicate addition and *assume* the other instructions? For example, one way to view addition is as an algebraic expression:

$$C = A + B$$

Why not allow a programmer to write statements in a form similar to algebraic expressions, read those source statements into a program, and let the program generate the necessary machine-level code (*Fig. 7.4*)? That's exactly what happens with a **compiler**. Compare the binary instructions in Figs. 7.3 and 7.4; they're identical.

Many compiler languages, including FORTRAN, BASIC, Pascal, PL/1, and ALGOL, are algebraically based. The most popular business-oriented language, COBOL, calls for statements that resemble brief English-language sentences (*Fig. 7.5*). Note, however, that no matter what language is used, the objective is the same. The programmer writes source code. An assembler program accepts mnemonic source code and generates a machine-level object module. A FORTRAN compiler accepts FORTRAN source code and generates a machine-level object module. A COBOL compiler accepts COBOL source code and generates a machine-level object module.

What's the difference between an assembler and a compiler? With an assembler, each source statement is converted to a single machine-level instruction. With a compiler, a given source statement may be converted to any number of machine-level instructions.

Fig. 7.4 A compile reads a programmer's source statements, translates each one to one or more machine-level instructions, and then combines them to form an object module.

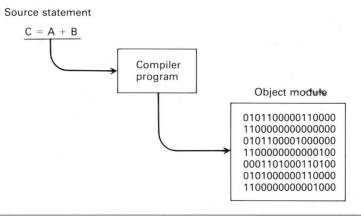

Source statement

C = A + B

Compiler program

Object module

```
0101100000110000
1100000000000000
0101100001000000
1100000000000100
0001101000110100
0101000000110000
1100000000001000
```

Fig. 7.5 The most popular business-oriented language is COBOL. As with other compiler languages, COBOL statements are translated into a machine-level object module.

Source statement

ADD A, B GIVING C.

Cobol compiler

Object module

```
0101100000110000
1100000000000000
0101100001000000
1100000000000100
0001101000110100
0101000000110000
1100000000001000
```

An option is using an **interpreter**. An assembler or a compiler reads a complete source program and generates a complete object module. An interpreter, on the other hand, works with one source statement at a time, reading it, translating it to machine-level, executing the resulting binary instructions, and then moving on to the next source statement. Both compilers and interpreters generate machine-level instructions, but the process is different.

Each language has its own syntax, punctuation, and spelling rules; for example, a Pascal source program is meaningless to a COBOL compiler or a BASIC interpreter. They all support writing programs, however. No matter what language is used, the programmer's objective is the same: defining a series of steps to guide the computer through some process.

Nonprocedural Languages

With traditional assemblers, compilers, and interpreters, the programmer defines a procedure telling the computer exactly how to solve a problem. However, with a modern, **nonprocedural language** (sometimes called a 4th-generation or declarative language), the programmer simply defines the logical structure of the problem and lets the language translator figure out how to solve it. Examples of commercially available nonprocedural languages include Prolog, Focus, Lotus 1-2-3, and many others. They are becoming increasingly popular.

Libraries

Picture a programmer writing a large program. As source statements are typed, they are manipulated by an editor program and stored on disk. Because large programs are rarely written in a single session, the programmer will eventually stop working and remove the disk from the drive. Later, when work resumes, the disk is reinserted, and new source statements are added to the old ones. That same disk might hold other source programs and even routines written by other programmers. It's a good example of a source statement **library** (*Fig. 7.6*).

Fig. 7.6   Source statements are typically typed, manipulated by an editor, and stored on a source statement library. If changes are necessary, the programmer can read the original statements from the library, change or delete them, add new statements, and update the library. Eventually, the source statements are compiled and an object module is created.

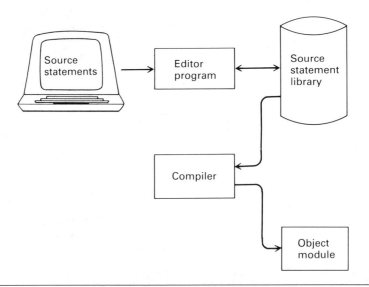

Eventually, the source program is completed and compiled. The resulting object module might be loaded directly into main memory, but more often, it is stored on an object module library (*Fig. 7.7*). Because object modules are binary, machine-level routines, there is no inherent difference between one produced by an assembler and one produced by a FORTRAN compiler (or any other compiler for that matter). Thus, object modules generated by different source languages can be stored on the same library.

Some object modules can be loaded into memory and executed. Others, however, include references to subroutines that are not part of the object module. For example, imagine a program that allows a computer to simulate a game of cards. If, some time ago, another programmer wrote an excellent subroutine to deal cards, it would make sense to reuse that logic.

Picture the new program after it has been written, compiled, and stored on the object module library (*Fig. 7.8*). The subroutine that deals cards is stored on the same library. Before the program is loaded, the two routines must be combined to form a **load module**. An object module is a machine-language translation of a source module, and may include references to other subroutines. A load module is a complete, ready to execute program with all subroutines in place. Combining object modules to form a load module is the job of the linkage editor or loader (*Fig. 7.8*).

Fig. 7.7 Object modules can be stored on a library, too. Because an object module is a binary, machine-level routine, there is no inherent difference between one produced by an assembler and one produced by a FORTRAN compiler, so both can be stored on the same library.

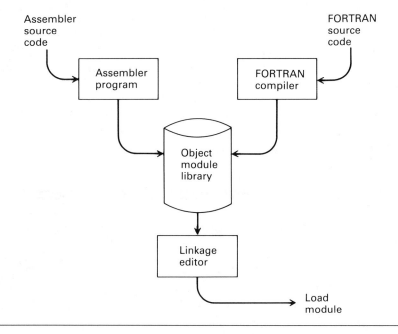

Fig. 7.8 A linkage editor or loader reads object modules from a library and combines them to form a load module.

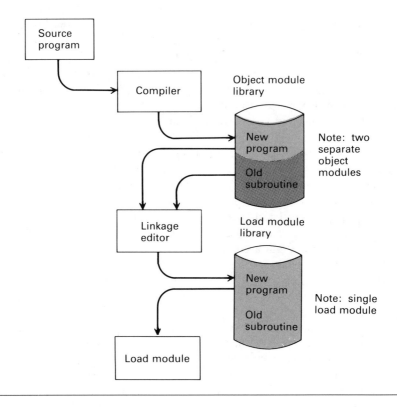

Video games, spreadsheet programs, word processors, database programs, accounting routines, and other commercial software packages are generally purchased on disk in load module form. Given a choice between source code, object modules, and load modules, most people would find the load module easier to use simply because the computer can execute it without translation. Load modules are difficult to change, however. If a programmer plans to modify or customize a software package, the source code is essential.

The Program Development Process

How does a programmer go about modifying a software package? More generally, how does a professional programmer go about the task of writing an original program? Programming is not quite a science; there is a touch of art involved. Thus it is not surprising that different programmers work in different ways. Most, however, begin by carefully defining the problem, and then planning their solution in detail before writing the code. Let's briefly investigate the program development process.

Problem Definition

The first step is defining the problem. That seems like common sense, but all too often, programs are written without a clear idea of why they are needed. A solution, even a great solution, to the wrong problem is useless.

Programs are written because people need information; thus, the programmer begins by identifying the desired information. Next, the algorithms, or rules, for generating that information are specified. Given the desired information (output) and the algorithms, the necessary input data can be defined. The result is a clear **problem definition** that gives the programmer a good idea of what the program must accomplish.

Incidentally, programs are usually defined in the context of a system. We'll consider systems analysis and design in Chapter 9.

Planning

The algorithms define what must be done; the next task is deciding how to do it. The objective is to state a problem solution in terms the computer can understand. A computer can perform arithmetic, compare, copy, and request input or output; thus, the programmer is limited to these basic operations. A good starting point is solving a small version of the problem; by actually solving the algorithm, even on a limited scale, the programmer can gain a good sense of the steps required to program it.

Programmers use a number of tools to help convert a problem solution to computer terms. For example, flowcharts can graphically represent a program's logic. With pseudocode the programmer can "draft" the logic before converting it to source code. More complex programs are often written by two or more programmers, or involve a great deal of logic. Such programs are typically broken down into smaller, single-function modules that can be independently coded. A good programmer plans the contents of each module and carefully defines the relationships between the modules before starting to write the source code. Just as a contractor prepares detailed blueprints before starting to build a house, a programmer develops a detailed program plan before starting to write code.

Writing the Program

During implementation, the programmer translates the problem solution into a series of source statements written in some programming language. While each programming language has its own syntax, punctuation, and spelling rules, and learning a new language takes time, writing instructions is basically a mechanical task. The real secret to programming isn't simply coding instructions; it's knowing what instruction to code next. That requires logic. Fortunately, knowing how to program is not a prerequisite for using a computer.

Debug and Documentation

Once the program is coded, the programmer must **debug** it. Often, the first step is correcting mechanical errors such as incorrect punctuation or spelling; the compiler or interpreter usually spots them. Much more difficult is finding and correcting logical errors, or **bugs**, that result from coding the wrong instruction. Valid instructions are not enough; they must be the right instructions in the right order. Once again, careful planning is the key; good planning simplifies program debug.

Program **documentation** consists of diagrams, comments, and other descriptive materials that explain or clarify the code. Documentation is invaluable during program debug, and essential for efficient program maintenance. Most useful are comments that appear in a program listing and explain the logic.

Maintenance

Once a program is completed, **maintenance** begins. Since it is impossible to test many large programs exhaustively, bugs can slip through the debug stage, only to show up months and even years later. Fixing such bugs is an important maintenance task. More significant is the need to update a program to keep it current; for example, because income tax rates change frequently, a payroll program must be constantly updated. The keys to maintenance are careful planning, good documentation, and good program design.

Writing Your Own Programs

Playing an instrument is not essential to enjoying music. Likewise, knowing how to program is not a prerequisite to using a computer. Most computer users can't program.

Still, just as a rudimentary knowledge of an instrument increases your appreciation for music, knowing how to program can make you a more effective computer user. Of course, it goes without saying that if you hope to earn your living as a computer professional, a knowledge of programming is essential. Some people find programming easy. Others find it extremely difficult. The key is practice. The only way to learn how to program *is* to program.

This book was *not* designed to teach programming. It does, however, lay a solid foundation for learning. An introduction to programming should be the next step in your education.

Summary

A program is a series of instructions that guides a computer through a process. Each instruction tells the machine to perform one of its basic functions. Because computers are binary machines, the program stored in a computer's main memory must be in binary form. Few programmers actually write machine-level instructions, however.

An assembler language programmer writes one mnemonic instruction for each machine-level instruction. An assembler program then reads the source statements, translates them to binary, and generates an object module. A compiler reads source statements, translates each one into one or more machine-level instructions, and then combines them to form an object module. An interpreter works with one source statement at a time, translating it and executing the resulting machine-level code before moving on to the next instruction. With a traditional compiler, interpreter, or assembler, the programmer defines a complete procedure for solving a problem. With a modern nonprocedural language, the programmer simply defines the logical structure of the problem and lets the translator program figure out how to solve it.

As programs are written, the source code is stored on a source statement library. The assembler or compiler reads the source code and stores the resulting object module on an object module library. A linkage editor or loader combines object modules to form a load module. An object module is a machine-level translation of a programmer's source code that may include references to other subroutines. A load module is a complete, ready to execute program.

The process of writing an original program begins with problem definition. The programmer's objective is to identify the desired information, determine the algorithms needed to generate that information, and then define the input data that drive the algorithms. Next comes planning, when the basic logical steps needed to solve the problem are determined.

Writing a program involves carefully translating the plan to a programming language. The process of removing errors (or bugs) from a program is called debugging. Once a program is completed, maintenance begins. Program debug and maintenance are simplified by good documentation.

After finishing this book, the next phase in your education should be learning to program. The only way to learn to program is to program.

Key Words

- assembler
- bug
- compiler
- debug
- documentation
- instruction
- interpreter

- library
- load module
- machine language
- maintenance
- nonprocedural language

- object module
- problem definition
- program
- source code

Self Test

1. During a single machine cycle, the processor fetches and executes
   _____ .

   a. one instruction   c. one statement
   b. several instructions   d. several statements

2. The program that actually controls a computer must be stored in main
   memory in _____ form.

   a. hexadecimal   c. logical
   b. binary   d. sequential

3. When using a(n) _____, a programmer writes one instruction
   for each machine-level instruction.

   a. assembler   c. compiler
   b. interpreter   d. program generator

4. Programmers write _____ code.

   a. object   c. machine-level
   b. source   d. load module

5. Compilers and assemblers read a programmer's code and generate
   _____ .

   a. an object module   c. a load module
   b. subroutines   d. source statements

6. When using _____ , each source statement is converted to one
   or more machine-level instructions.

   a. a compiler   c. an assembler
   b. machine code   d. an object module

7. When using a(n) _____ , a single source statement is read, immediately translated to machine-level, and then executed before the next
   source statement is read.

   a. compiler   c. assembler
   b. interpreter   d. nonprocedural language

8. When using a(n) _____ , a programmer simply defines the logical structure of a problem.

a. compiler
b. interpreter

c. assembler
d. nonprocedural language

9. A programmer's code is stored on a(n) _____ .

a. source library
b. load library

c. object library
d. user library

10. A linkage editor combines _____ modules to form a(n) _____ module.

a. source/object
b. source/load

c. object/load
d. object/source

11. The first step in the program development process is _____ .

a. problem definition
b. analysis

c. planning
d. coding

12. Problem definition begins with the desired _____ .

a. information (output)
b. data (input)

c. logic
d. algorithms

13. The process of removing errors from a program is called _____ .

a. documentation
b. debugging

c. compilation
d. maintenance

14. The diagrams, comments, and other descriptive materials that explain a programmer's code are called _____ .

a. source code
b. object code

c. documentation
d. an algorithm

15. Once a program is completed, _____ begins.

a. documentation
b. debug

c. maintenance
d. coding

Answers:

1.a 2.b 3.a 4.b 5.a 6.a 7.b 8.d 9.a 10.c 11.a 12.a 13.b 14.c 15.c

Relating the Concepts

1. Without a program to provide control, a computer is little more than an expensive calculator. Do you agree? Why, or why not?

2. Relate the idea of an instruction to a computer's basic machine cycle.

3. Why are programming languages necessary?

4. Distinguish between an assembler and a compiler.

5. Distinguish between a compiler and an interpreter.

6. What is a library? Why are libraries useful?

7. Distinguish between a source module, an object module, and a load module.

8. List the steps in the program development process, and briefly explain what happens during each step.

9. Developing a program involves a methodical, step-by-step process. Why?

10. The only way to learn to program is to program. Why?

8.

Data Management

KEY CONCEPTS

Why data management?

Accessing data
- Data structures
- Locating files
- Locating records
- The relative record concept

Access methods

Database management

Why Data Management?

We have already considered hardware and software in some detail. In this chapter, we turn our attention to a third basic computer resource, **data**. Many computer applications require that data be stored for subsequent processing. Simply storing the data is not enough, however. A typical computer system, even a small one, can have dozens of disks and tapes, each holding data for dozens of different applications. For any given application, one and only one set of data will do. We must be able to store, locate, and retrieve the specific data needed by a given program. That is the concern of **data management**.

Accessing Data

Imagine a single diskette containing several programs. For a particular application, only one of those programs will do. How is a given program selected, loaded, and executed? In Chapter 6, we learned that the operating system, responding to a user's command, reads the disk's index, searches it for the requested program name, extracts the program's track and sector address, and issues primitive commands to read it into main memory. Later, following a RUN command, the program is given control of the processor.

Accessing data presents a similar problem. A single diskette can hold data for several different applications. For a given application, one and only one set of data will do, and finding the right data is much like finding the right program. There are differences between accessing programs and accessing data, however. When a program is needed, all its instructions must be loaded into memory. Data, on the other hand, are typically processed *selectively*, a few elements at a time. Thus, it is not enough merely to locate the data; we must be able to distinguish the individual **data elements**, too.

Data Structures

The key to retrieving data is remembering where they are stored. If the data elements are stored according to a consistent and well understood structure, it is possible to retrieve them by remembering that structure.

The simplest **data structure** is a **list**. For example, data for a program that computes an average might be stored as a series of numbers separated by commas (*Fig. 8.1*). The commas distinguish the individual data elements.

Most programming languages support a more complex data structure called an **array** (*Fig. 8.2*). Each array element can hold one data value. Each element is assigned a unique identifying number or numbers, and individual data elements can be inserted, extracted, or manipulated by referencing those numbers. For example, in the array pictured in Fig. 8.2, elements are identified by a row number and a column number, and row 1, column 3 (element 1,3) contains the value 29. Once an array has been filled, it can be written to disk, tape, or any other secondary medium, and later read back into memory for processing.

Consider a program that generates name and address labels. For each label, we need a name, a street address, a city, a state, and a zip code. If we needed only a few labels, we might store the data in a list, but separating the elements would soon become tedious. An option is to set up an array of names and addresses, with each row holding the data for a single label. The only problem is that the entire array must be in main memory before the individual elements can be accessed, and main memory space is limited. Thus, even with an array, we could generate relatively few labels.

A better solution is to organize the data as a file (*Fig. 8.3*). All computer data begin as patterns of bits. On a file, the bits are grouped to form characters. Groups of characters, in turn, form meaningful data elements called **fields**. A group of related fields is a **record**; the **file** is a set of related records. For example, in a name and address file, an individual's name is a field. Each record holds a complete set of data for a single individual (a name, a street address, and so on). The file consists of all the records.

Fig. 8.1 The simplest data structure is a list. Separators, such as these commas, serve to distinguish individual values. Often, a "sentinel" value, such as a negative number, marks the end of the list.

4410, 843, 184, 31, 905, 6357, 44, 7702, 228, 59, −1

Fig. 8.2 Most programming languages support a more complex data structure called an array. Individual cells are assigned a number or numbers, and data values are inserted, manipulated, and extracted by referencing those numbers.

1,1	1,2	1,3	1,4	1,5
71	38	29	90	70
2,1	2,2	2,3	2,4	2,5
91	13	56	77	20
3,1	3,2	3,3	3,4	3,5
68	18	54	63	56
4,1	4,2	4,3	4,4	4,5
12	38	68	39	74
5,1	5,2	5,3	5,4	5,5
82	80	35	98	61

Fig. 8.3   Characters are grouped to form fields. Fields are grouped to form records. A file is a group of related records.

Name	Street address	City	State	Zip code
Melinda Atkins	142 Maple St.	Oxford	Ohio	450781718
Charles Baker	713 Main Street	Cincinnati	Ohio	457033304
Thomas Bates	42 South Blvd.	Atlanta	Georgia	352170315
Lisa Campanella	8 Tower Square	San Jose	California	953214450
Shen Chan	State Route 77	Binghamton	New York	127561495
Tomas Garcia	473 Dixie Highway	Lexington	Kentucky	434101236
⋮	⋮	⋮	⋮	⋮
Arthur White	Northside Mall	Orlando	Florida	214504372
Character				
Field	Field	Field	Field	Field
Record				

File {

The data in a file are processed record by record. Normally, the file is stored on a secondary medium such as disk. Programs are written to read a record, process its fields, generate the appropriate output, and then read and process another record. Because only one record is in main memory at a time, very little memory is needed. Because many records can be stored on a single disk, a great deal of data can be processed in this limited space.

Locating Files

Imagine a file stored on disk. The first step in accessing its data is finding the file. The task is much like finding a program, but there are differences. Following a command such as LOAD or RUN, programs are loaded by the operating system. Data, on the other hand, are processed by application programs, *in the context* of a program's logic. Typically, just before the data are required, the program asks the operating system to **open** the file. Each file has a name; the open logic (*Fig. 8.4*) reads the disk index, searches it by name, and finds the address of the first record in the file.

Locating Records

Once a file has been located, the process of accessing its records can begin. When a program needs input data, it reads a record; when it is ready to output results, it writes a record. Note that these instructions deal with selected records, not with the entire file. We open files. We read and write records.

Fig. 8.4   When a file is opened, the disk index is read into main memory and searched for the desired file's name. If the file name is found, the file's start address is extracted from the index.

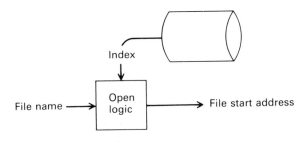

Fig. 8.5   Programmers think in terms of logical I/O. A physical device responds to primitive physical commands. In some way, logical I/O requests must be translated to physical commands.

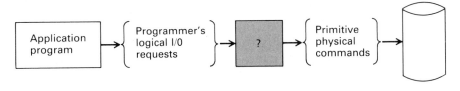

Let's examine the data accessing process more closely. A programmer views data logically, requesting the next record, or the name and address for a *particular* customer. The data are stored on a secondary medium such as disk. To access a record physically, the disk drive must be given a set of primitive commands: seeks, reads, and writes. The programmer thinks in terms of **logical I/O**. The external device stores and retrieves physical sectors; it "thinks" in terms of **physical I/O**. There must be a mechanism for translating the programmer's logical requests to the appropriate physical commands (*Fig. 8.5*). On small computers, much of the logic is found in the operating system's input/output control system; on larger machines, access methods are used. Increasingly, the programmer's logical data request is translated to physical form by a database management system.

The Relative Record Concept

How does software, be it operating system, access method, or database software, find specific records in a file? The key to many storage and retrieval techniques is the **relative record number**. Imagine a string of 100 records. Number the first one 0, the second 1, the third 2, and so on. The numbers indicate a given record's position relative to the first record in the file. The file's first record (relative record 0) is at "start of file plus 0"; its second record is at "start of file plus 1," and so on.

Now, store the records on disk (*Fig. 8.6*); to keep our initial example simple, we'll store one per sector. Number the sectors relative to the start of the file—0, 1, 2, and so on. Note that the relative record number, a logical concept, and the relative sector number, a physical location, are identical. Given a relative record number, it is possible to compute a relative sector number. Given a relative sector number, it is possible to compute a physical address on disk.

Fig. 8.6   A relative record number indicates a record's position relative to the first record in a file. Relative sector numbers are generated by counting from the physical file's first sector. Given a relative record number, it is possible to compute a physical disk address.

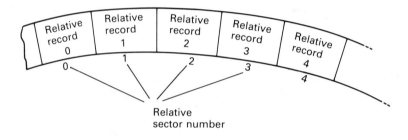

Fig. 8.7   Given the start of a file address (from open) and a relative record number, a physical disk address can be computed.

Relative record number	Actual location on disk	
	Track	Sector
0	30	0
1	30	1
2	30	2
3	30	3
4	30	4
5	30	5
6	30	6
7	30	7
8	30	8
9	30	9
10	30	10
⋮	⋮	⋮

Assume a file begins at track 30, sector 0, and that one logical record is stored in each sector. As Fig. 8.7 shows, relative record 0 is stored at track 30, sector 0; relative record 1 is at track 30, sector 1; and so on. Where is relative record 10? It must be stored at track 30, sector 10. In our example, the relative record number indicates how many sectors away from the beginning of the file the record is stored. Thus, we can compute the physical location of any record by adding its relative record number to the start-of-file address (which, remember, was extracted from the disk's index when the file was opened). The file starts at track 30, sector 0. Relative record 10 is stored 10 sectors away, at track 30, sector 10. To read record 10, the disk drive must be told to seek to track 30 and read sector 10. We have translated a logical data request to specific physical commands.

We might complicate matters by storing two or more logical records in each sector, or by creating a file extending over two or more tracks. While we won't discuss the details, in either case it is still possible to develop a simple algorithm to compute a record's physical location, given its relative record number. Many different algorithms are used. Some allow records to be stored or retrieved sequentially. Others allow individual records to be accessed in random order. Let's examine a few common data access techniques.

Access Methods

Imagine preparing meeting announcements for a club. You need a set of mailing labels, and each member's name and address is recorded on an index card. Probably the easiest way to generate the labels is to copy the data from the first card, turn to the second card and copy it, and so on, processing the records sequentially, from the beginning of the file to the end.

Magazine publishers face the same problem with each new issue, but need mailing labels for tens of thousands of subscribers. Rather than using index cards, they store customer data on disk or magnetic tape, one record per subscriber. The easiest way to ensure that all labels are generated is to process the records in the order in which they are stored, proceeding sequentially from the first record in the file to the last. To simplify handling, the records might be presorted by zip code or a mailing zone, but the basic idea of processing the data in physical order still holds.

How does this relate to the relative record number concept? A relative record number indicates a record's position on the file. With **sequential access**, processing begins with relative record 0, then moves to relative record 1, 2, and so on. Accessing data sequentially involves little more than counting. For example, imagine a program has just finished processing relative record 14. What is the next record? Obviously, relative record 15. We've already seen how a relative record number can be converted to a physical address; simply by counting records, it is possible to read them, or write them, in physical order.

Processing records in sequence is not always acceptable. For example, when a subscriber moves, his or her address must be changed in the file.

Searching for that subscriber's record sequentially is like looking for a telephone number by starting with the first page of the telephone book and reading line by line. That's not how we use a telephone book. Instead, knowing the records are stored in alphabetical order, we quickly narrow our search to a portion of a single page, and *then* begin reading the entries, ignoring the bulk of the data. The way we use a telephone book is a good example of **direct**, or **random, access**.

A disk drive reads or writes one record at a time. To randomly access a specific record, all the programmer must do is remember its address, and ask for it. The problem is remembering all those disk addresses. One solution is maintaining an **index** of the records. Again, we'll use the name and address file as an example. We want to access individual customer records by name. As the file is created, records are written, one at a time, in relative record number order. Additionally, as each record is written, the customer name and the associated relative record number are recorded in an array or index (*Fig. 8.8*). After the last record has been written to disk and its position recorded on the index, the index is itself stored.

Once the index has been created, it can be used to find individual records. Assume, for example, that Susan Smith has changed her address. To record her new address on the file, a program could:

1. read the file index,
2. search the index for her name,
3. find her relative record number,
4. compute the disk address, and read her record,
5. change her address, and
6. rewrite the record to the same place on disk.

Note that this specific record is accessed *directly*, and that no other records in the file are involved.

Fig. 8.8   A file index can help when records must be accessed directly.

Key	Relative record
Atkins, Melinda	0
Baker, Charles	1
Bates, Tomas	2
Campanella, Lisa	3
Chan, Shen	4
Garcia, Thomas	5
.	.
.	.
.	.

Fig. 8.9 Access methods translate a programmer's logical I/O requests to physical commands.

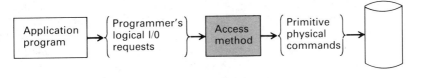

The basic idea of direct access is assigning each record an easy-to-remember, logical key, and then converting that key to a relative record number. Given this relative location, a physical address can be computed, and the record accessed. Using an index is one technique for converting keys to physical addresses. An option is passing a numeric key to an algorithm and computing a relative record number. Both techniques have the same objective: converting a programmer's logical data requests to physical form.

Earlier in the chapter (*Fig. 8.5*), we identified the gap separating logical and physical I/O. An **access method** is a software module that bridges this gap (*Fig. 8.9*), converting logical keys to physical addresses, and issuing the appropriate primitive commands. There are many variations of sequential, indexed, and direct organizations, and each one has its own access rules. Using a variety of data access techniques can be confusing, and this is one reason for the growing popularity of database management systems.

Database Management

There are problems with traditional data management. Many result from viewing applications independently. For example, consider payroll. Most organizations prepare their payrolls by computer because using a machine instead of a small army of clerks saves money. Thus, the firm develops a payroll program to process a payroll file. Inventory, accounts receivable, accounts payable, and general ledger analysis are similar applications, so the firm develops an inventory program, an inventory file, an accounts receivable program, an accounts receivable file, and so on. Each program is independent, and each processes its own independent data file.

Why is this a problem? For one thing, different applications often need the same data elements. For example, schools generate both bills and student grade reports. View the applications independently. The billing program reads a file of billing data, and the grade report program reads an independent file of grade data. The outputs of both programs are mailed to each student's home; thus, student names and addresses must be redundantly recorded on *both* files. What happens when a student moves? Unless both files are updated, one will be wrong. **Redundant data** are difficult to maintain.

A more subtle problem is **data dependency**. Each access method has its own rules for storing and retrieving data, and certain "tricks of the trade" can significantly improve the efficiency of a given program. Because the motivation for using the computer is saving money, the programmer is often tempted to save even more by taking advantage of these efficiencies. Thus, the program's logic becomes dependent upon the physical structure of the data. When a program's logic is tied to its physical data structure, changing that structure will almost certainly require changing the program. As a result, programs using traditional access methods can be difficult to maintain.

The solution to both problems is often organizing the data as a single, integrated **database**. The task of controlling access to all the data can then be concentrated in a centralized **database management system** (*Fig. 8.10*).

How does the use of a centralized database solve the data redundancy problem? All data are collected and stored in a single place; consequently, there is one and only one copy of any given data element. When the value of an element (an address, for example) changes, the single database copy is corrected. Any program requiring access to this data element gets the same value, because there *is* only one value.

How does a database help to solve the data dependency problem? Since the responsibility for accessing the physical data rests with the database management system, the programmer can ignore the physical data structure. As a result, programs tend to be much less dependent upon their data, and are generally much easier to maintain. Expect the trend toward database management to continue.

Fig. 8.10   A database management system insulates the programmer from the physical data.

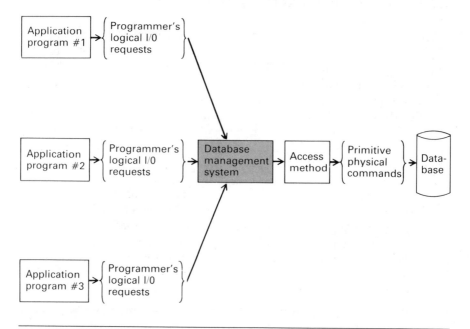

Summary

The focus of this chapter was data. Merely storing data is not enough; they must be stored in such a way that the individual data elements can be retrieved when needed. The key to retrieving data is remembering where they are stored. Often, the secret is storing them in a well-defined structure, and then retrieving them by remembering that structure. The simplest data structure is a list. Most programming languages support a more complex data structure called an array, with individual data elements identified by numbering the array's cells.

In a file, individual characters are grouped to form fields, fields are grouped to form records, and a set of related records forms the file. A file is located by asking the operating system to open it. When the open logic is executed, the disk index is searched for the file's name, and the track and sector address of the file's first record is extracted.

Accessing the data on a file involves reading and writing individual records. The programmer thinks in terms of logical I/O; hardware performs physical I/O. Software, in the form of the operating system's input/output control system, an access method, or a database management system, translates the logical requests into the necessary physical commands.

Often, the key to finding a specific record is its relative record number. The records in a file are numbered sequentially, with each relative record number indicating the record's position relative to the first one in the file. Given its relative record number, it is possible to compute a record's physical location.

A number of data access techniques are used to convert relative record numbers to physical record locations. With sequential access, the data are stored and retrieved in a fixed order, essentially by counting records. With direct or random access, individual records can be retrieved without regard for their positions on the physical file. Often, an index of the records is maintained. When a record is needed, the index is searched, the record's relative record number is extracted, a physical address is computed, and the record is read. Other direct access techniques compute a relative record number from a numeric key.

There are problems with traditional data management. Because different applications often require the same data, certain data elements may be stored in several different places, and such redundant data are difficult to maintain. Another problem is data dependency. If a program's logic is too closely linked to the physical structure of its data, that program can be difficult to maintain. The solution to both problems is often collecting all the organization's data in a centralized database. With a database, there is only one copy of each data element, so the data redundancy problem is eliminated. Because every program must access data through a database management system, programs are insulated from the physical data structure; thus, data dependency is reduced.

Key Words

- access method
- array
- data
- database
- database management system
- data dependency
- data element

- data management
- data structure
- direct access
- field
- file
- index
- list structure
- logical I/O
- open

- physical I/O
- random access
- record
- redundant data
- relative record number
- sequential access

Self-Test

1. The operating system locates a specific program by searching the disk's
   _____ .

   a. compiler
   b. boot

   c. table
   d. index

2. The simplest data structure is a(n) _____ .

   a. file
   b. list

   c. record
   d. array

3. Data values are accessed by element number (or numbers) in a(n)
   _____ .

   a. list
   b. array

   c. file
   d. record

4. A single, meaningful data element, such as a person's name, is a(n)
   _____ .

   a. record
   b. element

   c. field
   d. file

5. A group of related fields forms a(n) _____ .

   a. record
   b. file

   c. array
   d. list

6. A set of related records forms a(n) _____ .

a. field   c. list

b. array   d. file

7. The programmer thinks in terms of _____ .

    a. physical I/O   c. primitives

    b. logical I/O   d. commands

8. Transferring a single sector from disk into main memory is an example of _____ .

    a. physical I/O   c. file access

    b. logical I/O   d. a data structure

9. Given a _____ relative record number, it is possible to compute a _____ disk address.

    a. logical/physical   c. true/false

    b. physical/logical   d. false/true

10. A programmer's logical I/O requests are converted to physical commands by _____ .

    a. the program   c. the channel

    b. hardware   d. an access method

11. Records are processed in the order in which they are recorded under _____ processing.

    a. direct   c. sequential

    b. random   d. indexed

12. With _____ access, records can be accessed in any order.

    a. sequential   c. record

    b. file   d. direct

13. Data _____ occurs when the same data are stored in two or more files.

    a. redundancy   c. dependency

    b. access   d. loss

14. Data _____ occurs when a program's logic is closely tied to a physical data structure.

a. redundancy
b. access

c. loss
d. dependency

15. Data redundancy and data dependency can be avoided by using _____ .

a. a database
b. files

c. sequential files
d. random files

Answers

1.d 2.b 3.b 4.c 5.a 6.d 7.b 8.a 9.a 10.d 11.c 12.d 13.a 14.d 15.a

Relating the Concepts

1. When a program is accessed, all its instructions are accessed. Data, on the other hand, are accessed selectively. Explain.

2. What is a data structure? Why are data structures important?

3. Relate the terms character, field, record, and file.

4. What happens when a file is opened? Why?

5. Briefly explain the difference between logical I/O and physical I/O.

6. Briefly explain the relative record concept.

7. Distinguish between sequential access and direct access. Relate both access techniques to the relative record concept.

8. What is an access method? Why are access methods needed?

9. What is a database? Why are databases useful?

10. Relate a data base management system to an access method. How are they similar? How are they different?

9.

Systems Analysis and Design

Systems

Working under control of a stored program, a computer processes data into information. Think about that definition for a minute. Any given computer application involves at least three components: hardware, software, and data. Merely writing a program isn't enough, because the program is but one component in a system.

A **system** is a group of components that work together to accomplish an objective. For example, consider a payroll system. Its objective is paying employees. What components are involved? Each day, employees record their hours worked on time cards. At the end of each week, the time cards are collected and delivered to the computer center, where they are read into a payroll program. As it runs, the program accesses data files. Finally, the paychecks are printed and distributed. For the system to work, people, procedures, input and output media, files, hardware, and software must be carefully coordinated. Note that the program is but one component in a system.

Systems Analysis

Computer-based systems are developed because people need information. Those people, called **users**, generally know what is required, but may lack the expertise to obtain it. Technical professionals, such as programmers, have the expertise, but may lack training in the user's field. To complicate matters, users and programmers often seem to speak different languages, leading to communication problems. A **systems analyst** is a professional who translates user needs into technical terms (*Fig. 9.1*), thus serving as a bridge between users and technical professionals.

Like an engineer or an architect, a systems analyst solves problems by combining solid technical skills with insight, imagination, and a touch of art. Generally, the analyst follows a well-defined, methodical process that includes at least the following steps:

1. Problem definition
2. Analysis
3. Design
4. Implementation
5. Maintenance

Fig. 9.1   A systems analyst translates user needs into technical terms.

At the end of each step, results are documented and shared with both the user and the programmers. The idea is to catch and correct errors and misunderstandings as early as possible. Perhaps the best way to illustrate the process is through an example.

Picture a small clothing store that purchases merchandise at wholesale, displays this stock, and sells it to customers at retail. On the one hand, too much stock represents an unnecessary expense. On the other hand, a poor selection discourages shoppers. Ideally, a balance can be achieved: enough, but not too much.

Complicating matters is the fact that inventory is constantly changing, with customer purchases depleting stock, and returns and reorders adding to it. The owner would like to track inventory levels and reorder any given item just before the store runs out. For a single item, the task is easy—just count the stock-on-hand. Unfortunately, the store has hundreds of different items, and keeping track of each one is impractical. Perhaps a computer might help.

Problem Definition

The first step in the systems analysis and design process is **problem definition**. The analyst's objective is determining what the user (in this case, the store's owner) needs. Note that, as the process begins, the *user* possesses the critical information, and the analyst must listen and learn. Few users are technical experts. Most see the computer as a "magic box," and are not concerned with how it works. At this stage, the analyst has no business even *thinking* about programs, files, and computer hardware, but must communicate with the user on his or her own terms.

The idea is to ensure that both the user and the analyst are thinking about the same thing. Thus, a clear, written statement expressing the analyst's understanding of the problem is essential. The user should review and correct this written statement. The time to catch misunderstandings and oversights is now, before time, money, and effort are wasted.

Often, following a preliminary problem definition, the analyst performs a **feasibility study**. The study, a brief capsule version of the entire systems analysis and design process, attempts to answer three questions:

1. Can the problem be solved?

2. Can it be solved in the user's environment?

3. Can it be solved at a reasonable cost?

If the answer to any one of these questions is no, the system should *not* be developed. Given a good problem definition and a positive feasibility study, the analyst can turn to planning and developing a problem solution.

Analysis

As **analysis** begins, the analyst understands the problem. The next step is determining *what* must be done to solve it. The user knows what must be done; during analysis, this knowledge is extracted and formally documented. Most users think in terms of the functions to be performed and the data elements to be manipulated. The objective is to identify and link these key functions and data elements, yielding a **logical system** design.

Start with the system's basic functions. The key is keeping track of the stock-on-hand for each product in inventory. Inventory changes because customers purchase, exchange, and return products, so the system will have to process customer transactions. The store's owner wants to selectively look at the inventory level for any product in short supply and, if appropriate, order replacement stock, so the system must be able to communicate with management. Finally, following management authorization, the system should generate a reorder ready to send to a supplier.

Given the system's basic functions, the analyst's next task is gaining a sense of their logical relationship. A good way to start is by describing how data flow between the functions. As the name implies, **data flow diagrams** are particularly useful for graphically describing these data flows. Four symbols are used (*Fig. 9.2*). Data sources and destinations are represented by squares; input data enter the system from a source, and output data flow to a destination. Once in the system, the data are manipulated or changed by processes, represented by round-corner rectangles. A process might be a program, a procedure, or anything else that changes or moves data. Data can be held for later processing in data stores, symbolized by open-ended rectangles. A data store might be a disk file, a tape file, a database, written notes, or even a person's memory. Finally, data flow between sources, destinations, processes, and data stores over data flows, which are represented by arrows.

Fig. 9.2   A data flow diagram uses four symbols to represent the components of a logical system.

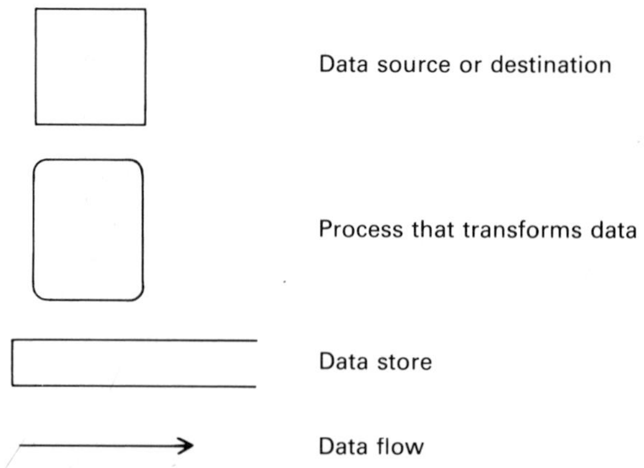

Data source or destination

Process that transforms data

Data store

Data flow

Figure 9.3 shows a preliminary data flow diagram for the inventory system. Start with *CUSTOMER*. Transactions flow from a customer, into the system, where they are handled by *Process transaction*. A data store, *STOCK*, holds data on each item in inventory. *Process transaction* changes the data to reflect the new transaction. Meanwhile, *MANAGEMENT* accesses the system through *Communicate*, evaluating the data in *STOCK* and, if necessary, requesting a reorder. Once a reorder is authorized, *Generate reorder* sends necessary data to the *SUPPLIER*, who ships the items to the store. Note that, because the reorder represents a change in the inventory level of a particular product or products, it is handled as a transaction.

The data flow diagram describes the logical system. The next step is tracing the data flows. Start with the destination *SUPPLIER*. Reorders flow to suppliers; for example, the store might want 25 pairs of jeans. To fill the order, the supplier needs the product description and the reorder quantity. Where do these data elements come from? Since they are output by *Generate reorder*, they must either be input to or generated by this process. Data flow into *Generate reorder* from *STOCK*; thus, product descriptions and reorder quantities must be stored in *STOCK*.

Other data elements, such as the item purchased and the purchase quantity, are generated by *CUSTOMER*. Still others, for example selling price and reorder point, are generated by or needed by *MANAGEMENT*. The current stock-on-hand for a given item is an example of a data element generated by an algorithm in one of the procedures. Step by step, methodically, the analyst identifies the data elements to be input to, stored by, manipulated by, generated by, or output by the system.

To keep track of the data elements, the analyst might list each one in a **data dictionary** (*Fig. 9.4*). A simple data dictionary can be set up on index cards, but computerized data dictionaries have become increasingly popular. The data dictionary, a collection of data describing and defining the data, is useful throughout the systems analysis and design process, and is often used to build a database during the implementation stage.

Fig. 9.3   A data flow diagram of the inventory system.

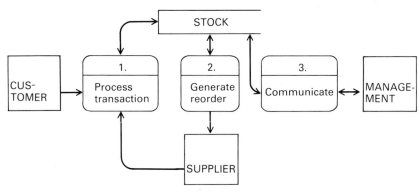

Fig. 9.4   Data elements are formally documented in a data dictionary.

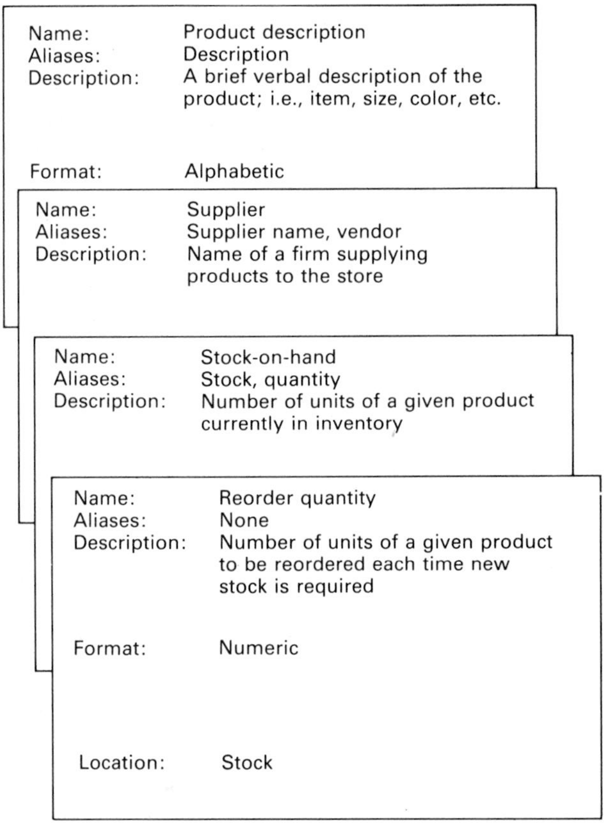

```
Name:          Product description
Aliases:       Description
Description:   A brief verbal description of the
               product; i.e., item, size, color, etc.


Format:        Alphabetic
```
```
Name:          Supplier
Aliases:       Supplier name, vendor
Description:   Name of a firm supplying
               products to the store
```
```
Name:          Stock-on-hand
Aliases:       Stock, quantity
Description:   Number of units of a given product
               currently in inventory
```
```
Name:          Reorder quantity
Aliases:       None
Description:   Number of units of a given product
               to be reordered each time new
               stock is required


Format:        Numeric



Location:      Stock
```

The idea of analysis is to define the system's major functions and data elements methodically. Remember that the objective is translating user needs into technical terms. Since the system starts with the user, the first step is defining the user's needs. Users think in terms of functions and data. They do *not* visualize programs, or files, or hardware, and during this initial, crucial analysis stage, it is essential that the analyst think like a user, not like a programmer.

Data flow diagrams and data dictionaries are useful tools. They provide a format for recording key information about the proposed system. Also, they jog the analyst's memory; for example, if the analyst doesn't have sufficient information to complete a data dictionary entry, he or she has probably missed something. Perhaps most importantly, the data flow diagram and the data dictionary document the analyst's understanding of the system requirements. By reviewing these documents, the user can correct misunderstandings or oversights. Finally, they represent an excellent starting point for the next step, design.

Design

As we enter the **design** stage, we know what the system must do, and thus can begin thinking about *how* to do it. The objective is to develop a strategy for solving the problem. At this stage, we are not interested in writing code or in defining precise data structures; instead, we want to identify, at a black box level, necessary programs, files, procedures, and other components.

The data flow diagram defines the system's necessary functions; how might they be implemented? One possibility is writing one program for each process. Another is combining two or more processes in a single program; there are dozens of alternative solutions. Let's focus on one option and document it.

A **system flowchart** uses symbols to represent programs, procedures, hardware devices, and the other components of a **physical system** (*Fig. 9.5*). Our flowchart (*Fig. 9.6*) shows that transaction data enter the system through a terminal, are processed by a data collection program, and then are stored on an inventory file. Eventually, the inventory file is processed by a *Report and reorder* program. Through it, management manipulates the data and authorizes reorders.

Fig. 9.5   On a system flowchart, symbols represent programs, procedures, hardware devices, and the other components of a physical system.

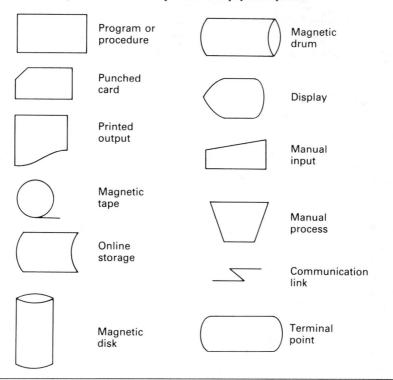

Fig. 9.6   A flowchart of the proposed physical system.

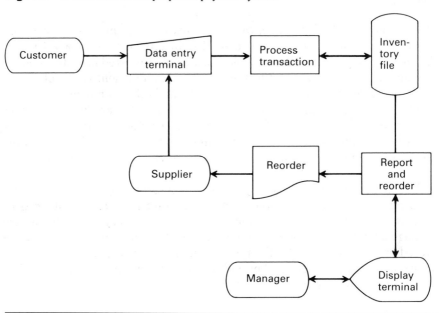

Look at the system flowchart. It identifies several hardware components, including a computer, a disk drive, a data entry terminal, a printer, and a display terminal. Two programs are needed: *Process transaction* and *Report and reorder*. In addition to the hardware and the programs, we'll need data structures for the inventory file and for data flows between the I/O devices and the software. Note that this system flowchart illustrates one possible solution; a good analyst will develop several feasible alternatives before choosing one.

The flowchart maps the system, highlighting its major physical components. Since the data link the components, the next task is defining the data structures. Consider, for example, the inventory file. It contains all the data elements from the data store *STOCK*. The data elements are listed in the data dictionary. Using them, the file's data structure can be planned.

How should the file be organized? That depends on how it will be accessed. For example, in some applications, data are processed at regular, predictable intervals. Typically, the data are collected over time and processed together, as a batch. If **batch processing** is acceptable, a sequential file organization is probably best.

It is not always possible to wait until a batch of transactions is collected, however. For example, consider an air defense early warning system. If an unidentified aircraft is spotted, it must be identified immediately; the idea of waiting until 5:00 p.m. because "that's when the air defense program is run" is absurd. Instead, because of the need for quick response, each transaction must be processed as it occurs. Generally, such **transaction processing** systems call for direct access files.

Our inventory system has two programs. One processes transactions. A direct access inventory file seems a reasonable choice. The other allows management to study inventory data occasionally; batch processing would certainly do. Should the inventory file be organized sequentially or directly? Faced with such a choice, a good analyst considers *both* options. One possible system might accept transactions and process them as they occur. As an alternative, sales slips might be collected throughout the day and processed as a batch after the store closes. In the first system, the two programs would deal with direct access files; in the second system, they would be linked to sequential files. A program to process direct access data is different from a program to process sequential data. The data drive the system. The choice of a data structure determines the program's structure. Note that the program is defined and planned *in the context* of the system.

Implementation

Once the system's major components have been identified, we can begin to develop them. Our system includes two programs, several pieces of equipment, and a number of data structures. During **implementation**, each program is planned and written using the techniques described in Chapter 7. Files are created, and their contents checked. New hardware is purchased, installed, and tested. Additionally, operating procedures are written and evaluated. Once all the component parts are ready, the system is tested. Assuming the user is satisfied, the finished system is released.

Maintenance

Maintenance begins after the system is released. As people use it, they will suggest minor improvements and enhancements. Occasionally, bugs slip through debug and testing, and removing them is another maintenance task. Finally, conditions change, and a program must be updated; for example, if the government passes a law changing the procedure for collecting income taxes, the payroll program must be modified. Maintenance continues for the life of a system, and its cost can easily match or exceed the original development cost. Good planning, solid documentation, and well-structured programs can help to minimize maintenance cost.

Summary

A system is a collection of hardware, software, data, and procedural components that work together to accomplish an objective. A program is but one component in a system.

Systems are planned and designed by systems analysts who generally follow a well-defined, methodical process. The first step in the process is problem definition, when the analyst attempts to discover exactly what the user needs. Often, following a preliminary problem definition, a feasibility study is conducted to determine if the problem can be solved.

Given a clear problem definition, analysis begins. During this stage, the analyst develops a logical model of the system. Key functions are linked through a data flow diagram. Using the diagram as a tool, the data flows are traced, and the system's data elements are identified and recorded in a data dictionary. After the logical system is reviewed with the user, design begins.

During design, the analyst develops a model of the physical system. A system flowchart can be used to map the system, defining each physical component as a symbol. A good systems analyst considers a number of alternative solutions to the problem before settling on one. Implementation follows design. Programs are planned and written; hardware is ordered and installed; procedures are written; files and databases are initialized; and, finally, the pieces are assembled and tested. Following release of the system, maintenance begins.

Key Words

- analysis
- batch processing
- data dictionary
- data flow diagram
- design
- feasibility study

- implementation
- logical system
- maintenance
- physical system
- problem definition
- system

- system flowchart
- systems analysis
- systems analyst
- transaction processing
- user

Self-Test

1. A _____ is one component in a _____ .

   a. system/program
   b. program/system
   c. system/computer
   d. computer/program

2. A professional who translates user needs into technical terms is a _____ .

   a. user
   b. systems analyst
   c. programmer
   d. manager

3. The first step in the systems analysis and design process is _____ .

a. feasibility study
b. analysis

c. problem definition
d. design

4. During problem definition, the _____ is the source of critical information.

a. user
b. systems analyst

c. programmer
d. manager

5. A systems analyst might conduct _____ to determine if a problem can be solved.

a. analysis
b. design

c. a feasibility study
d. problem definition

6. During analysis, the analyst plans a _____ .

a. system
b. physical system

c. logical system
d. feasibility study

7. A logical system design can be documented by a _____ .

a. flowchart
b. data flow diagram

c. system flowchart
d. data dictionary

8. During analysis, the analyst's objective is to identify the systems's _____ .

a. logical functions
b. data elements

c. both
d. neither

9. To keep track of data elements, an analyst might develop a _____ .

a. data dictionary
b. file

c. data flow diagram
d. system flowchart

10. Concern for the physical structure of the system begins during _____ .

a. analysis
b. design

c. implementation
d. problem definition

11. A physical system design can be mapped in a _____ .

a. flowchart
b. system flowchart

c. data flow diagram
d. data dictionary

12. Which file organization would you select for a batch processing application?

    a. direct   c. indexed
    b. random   d. sequential

13. Which file organization would you select for a transaction processing application?

    a. direct   c. either
    b. sequential   d. neither

14. Programs are written during _____ .

    a. implementation   c. maintenance
    b. design   d. analysis

15. After a system is "finished," _____ begins.

    a. implementation   c. maintenance
    b. debug   d. documentation

Answers

1.b 2.b 3.c 4.a 5.c 6.c 7.b 8.c 9.a 10.b 11.b 12.d 13.a 14.a
15.c

Relating the Concepts

1. What is a system?

2. Programs are defined and planned in the context of a system. Explain.

3. What does a systems analyst do? Why is someone like a systems analyst needed?

4. List the steps in the systems analysis and design process, and briefly explain what happens during each step.

5. During problem definition, the analyst must communicate with the user in the user's own terms. Why?

6. What is a feasibility study? What does the analyst hope to accomplish during a feasibility study?

7. Briefly explain the difference between a logical system and a physical system.

8. A systems analyst follows a methodical, step-by-step process when developing a system. Why?

9. Distinguish between batch processing and transaction processing.

10. A good systems analyst will consider several alternative physical system designs before selecting one. Why?

10.

Multiprogramming and Multiprocessing

KEY CONCEPTS

Multiprogamming

Multiprogramming operating systems
- Managing the processor's time
- Memory management
- I/O device allocation
- Scheduling
- Spooling

Time-sharing

Multiprocessing

Multiprogramming

Early computers were capable of executing a few thousand instructions per second. Modern mainframes are much faster, executing *millions* of instructions per second. Such speeds are difficult to imagine; let's just say that today's computers are very fast, indeed.

Unfortunately, the speeds of peripheral devices have not kept pace. Keyboards are driven by human beings; how fast can you type? Card readers, printers, and similar devices transmit, at best, a few thousand characters per second, and even "high-speed" secondary storage is a poor match for a computer. A modern mainframe is capable of processing data hundreds—even thousands—of times faster than its peripheral devices can supply them.

What does the computer do during input or output? Nothing. A program can't process data it doesn't yet have, and the success of an output operation can't be assumed until the operation is finished, so the program waits. Since the program controls the computer, the computer waits, too.

Because it is so much faster than its peripherals, a computer typically spends far more time waiting for input and output than it does processing data. During a single second, a large mainframe can execute a million instructions or more, so each unused second represents a tremendous waste of potential computing power. The problem is a bit like running a high-speed train on poorly maintained tracks. What good is speed you can't use?

Why not put two programs in main memory? Then, when program A is waiting for data, the processor can turn its attention to program B (*Fig. 10.1*). And why stop at two programs? With three, even more otherwise wasted time is utilized (*Fig. 10.2*). Generally, the more programs in memory, the greater the utilization of the processor. This technique is known as **multiprogramming**.

Fig. 10.1   With two programs in main memory, the processor can switch its attention to program B when program A is waiting for input or output.

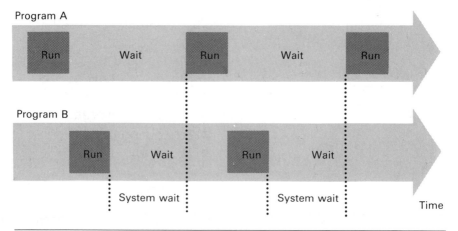

Fig. 10.2   More programs in main memory means that even more "wait" time can be utilized.

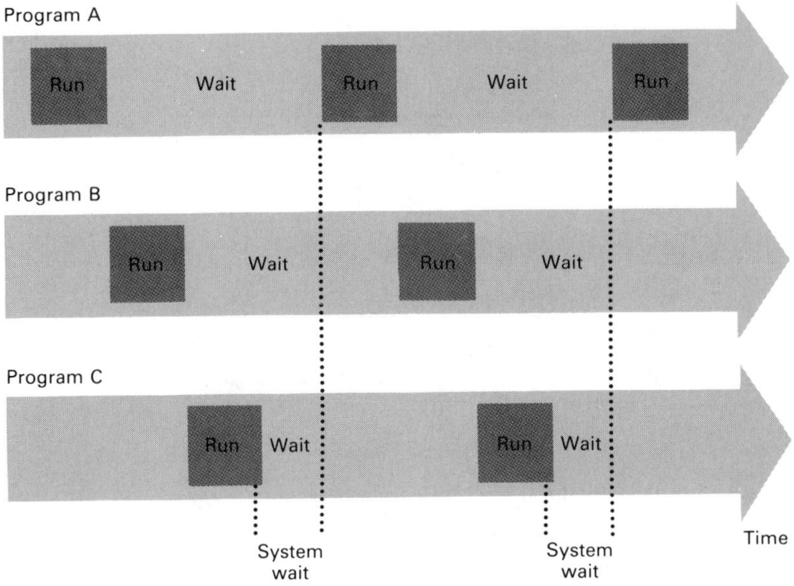

Program A

| Run | Wait | Run | Wait | Run |

Program B

| Run | Wait | Run | Wait |

Program C

| Run | Wait | Run | Wait |

System wait   System wait   Time

Note that, although several different programs are in main memory, the processor works on only one at a time. Why? The processor fetches and executes a *single* instruction during each machine cycle. If the processor can execute only one *instruction* at a time, it cannot possibly work on more than one *program* at a time. Simultaneous means "at the same instant." No one can study and watch television simultaneously. No processor can execute two or more programs simultaneously. **Concurrent** means "over the same time period." Some students can concurrently study and watch television. A processor can certainly execute two or more programs concurrently.

Multiprogramming Operating Systems

The advantages of multiprogramming are obvious: more programs can be run in the same amount of time on the same computer. However, while a computer's resources are substantial, they are limited and, with two or more concurrent users, conflicts over processor time, main memory space, and peripheral device allocations are inevitable. When these conflicts occur, they must be resolved. Since human operators cannot function at computer speeds, key decisions must be made by the computer itself. Because a computer's **operating system** serves as a hardware/software interface, its "in between" position makes it an ideal place to implement **resource management**.

Fig. 10.3   Most elementary operating systems contain a command processor and an input/output system. Multiprogramming operating systems are built on this base.

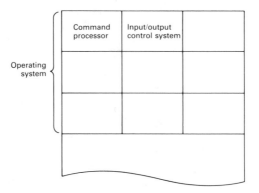

We first encountered operating systems in Chapter 6, where we studied two modules: the command processor and the input/output control system (*Fig. 10.3*). Because a mainframe is composed of so many components, its command processor and IOCS are more complex than a microcomputer's (for example, compare IBM's job control language to MS/DOS command language), but the functions performed are similar. A multiprogramming operating system builds on this base, adding modules to manage processor time, main memory space, and peripheral devices. Let's start with processor time.

Managing the Processor's Time

Imagine that two programs, A and B, are in memory. Some time ago, program A requested data from disk (*Fig. 10.4*). The input operation was assigned to a channel, and the processor turned to program B. Assume that the input operation has just been completed. *Both* programs are ready to run. Which one gets the processor?

Fig. 10.4   With multiple concurrent users, it is possible that two or more programs will be ready to execute at the same time. When this happens, an operating system module must resolve the conflict, deciding which program goes first.

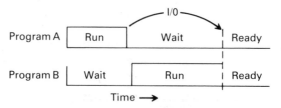

Fig. 10.5 The processor's time is managed by an operating system module.

	Command processor	Input/output control system	Processor management
Operating system {			

One possible solution is to display a message on the console asking the operator to make a decision. The operator will need at least a second or two to respond, and during that second or two, the processor could easily have executed instructions for *both* programs. Computers are so fast that a human being cannot effectively make such real-time choices. On most multiprogramming systems, the processor's time is managed by an operating system module (*Fig. 10.5*).

How does the operating system know when to switch from one program to another? The key is I/O. A program loses control of the processor when it starts an input or output operation and is eligible to regain control when that operation is complete. If the operating system is to decide which program goes next, it must know when input or output operations begin and end. Electronic signals called **interrupts** are used to mark these events. When an interrupt is sensed, no matter what the computer may be doing, hardware automatically transfers control to the operating system.

Follow the steps in *Fig. 10.6*. When an application program needs data, it issues an interrupt (*Fig. 10.6a*). In response, hardware transfers control to the operating system. Once it gets control, the operating system drops the application program into a **wait state** (*Fig. 10.6b*), starts the input or output operation, and gives control to another application program (*Fig. 10.6c*). Later, when the I/O operation is finished, the *channel* issues an interrupt (*Fig. 10.6d*). Once again the operating system gets control (*Fig. 10.6e*) and marks the program needing data "ready." Then, it transfers control to an application program (*Fig. 10.6f*).

The operating system uses an algorithm to decide which program goes next. For example, if all the programs are listed in a table in priority order, the operating system can scan this table after each interrupt and select the first "ready" program it encounters. Priority rules might be based on such criteria as a program's size, location in memory, time in memory, or the significance of the information it produces. The key point is that the priority decision is handled by the operating system at computer speed.

Fig. 10.6   The key to managing the processor's time is recognizing when input and output operations begin and end. Generally, these crucial events are signaled by interrupts.

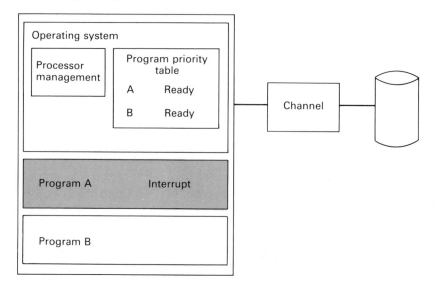

a.   When an application program needs data, it issues an interrupt.

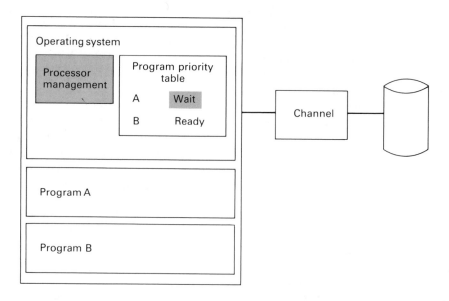

b.   Following the interrupt, the operating system gets control and sets the program to a wait state.

Fig. 10.6

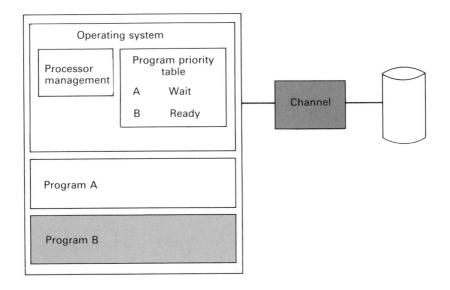

c. After starting the requested input or output operation the operating system gives control to another application program.

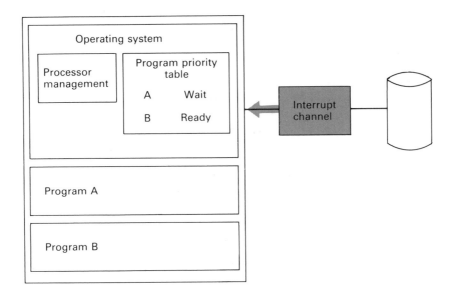

d. Eventually, the channel signals the end of the I/O operation by sending the computer an interrupt.

Fig. 10.6

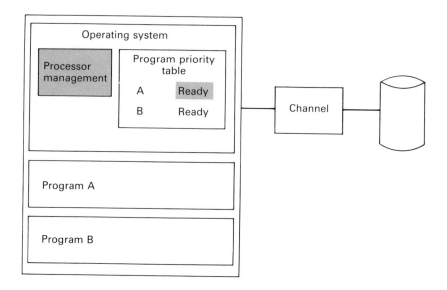

e. Following the interrupt, the operating system gets control and resets program A to a ready state.

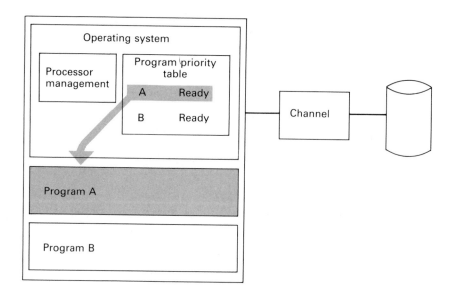

f. Finally, the operating system selects an application program and gives it control of the processor.

Memory Management

Memory management is concerned with allocating main memory space to application programs; like **processor management**, it is the responsibility of the operating system (*Fig 10.7*). The simplest approach, **fixed partition memory management** (*Fig. 10.8*), divides the available space into fixed-length partitions, and stores one program in each. More efficient memory utilization is achieved with **dynamic memory management**. Using this technique, the available memory is treated as a large pool of free space, and each program is assigned exactly as much as it needs.

Fig. 10.7 Memory management is another operating system responsibility.

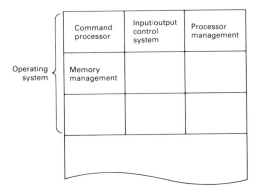

Fig. 10.8 Under fixed partition memory management, the available main memory space is divided into a series of fixed-length partitions.

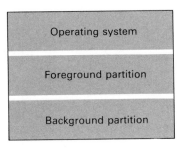

If a computer can execute only one instruction at a time, why must an entire program be loaded into main memory? Why not load only the active parts? On **virtual memory** systems, application programs are placed on secondary storage, and portions are moved into main memory as needed (*Fig. 10.9*). These "partial" programs require less memory space than would complete programs. Since less space is needed for each program, more programs can be loaded into main memory. More programs mean more efficient utilization of the processor.

Fig. 10.9 On a virtual memory system, portions of programs move back and forth between main memory and secondary storage.

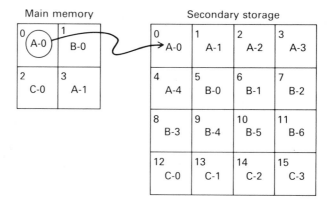

a. An unneeded portion of a program is copied to secondary storage.

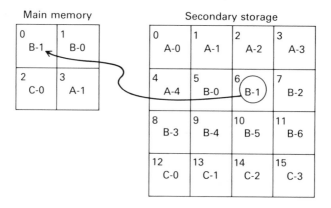

b. A needed portion of another program replaces it in main memory.

Fig. 10.10   The operating system also allocates input, output, and secondary storage devices, enqueues programs, schedules programs for loading into main memory, and performs a number of other support functions.

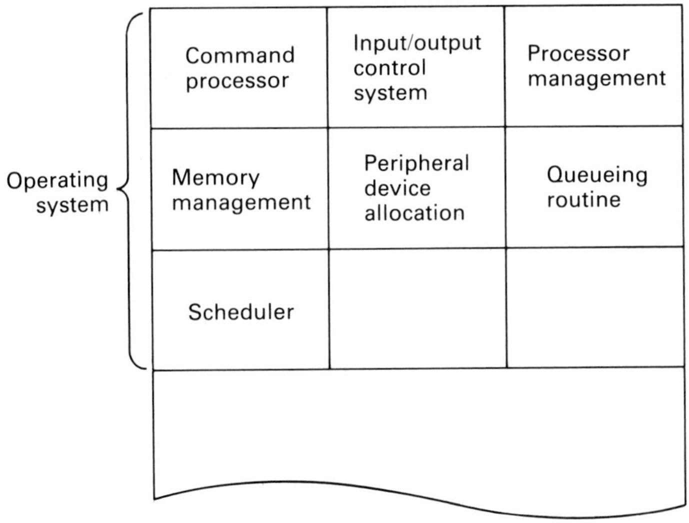

Command processor	Input/output control system	Processor management
Memory management	Peripheral device allocation	Queueing routine
Scheduler		

Operating system

I/O Device Allocation

What would happen if two programs were to take turns writing to the same printer? The output would be useless. Or, imagine programs *A* and *B* taking turns writing and reading data to and from the same tape. The result would be chaos! This cannot be allowed to happen; access to I/O devices must be carefully managed. Once again, the operating system is responsible (*Fig. 10.10*).

Scheduling

Processor management is concerned with the internal priorities of programs already in main memory. As a program finishes processing and space becomes available, which program is loaded into memory next? This decision typically involves two separate modules, a job **queueing** routine and a **scheduling** routine (*Fig. 10.10*).

As programs enter the system, they are placed on a queue by the job queueing routine (*Fig. 10.11*). When space becomes available, the scheduler selects a program from the queue and loads it into main memory (*Fig. 10.12*). Often, the first program on the queue is the first one loaded; frequently, more sophisticated priority rules are used to determine which program is loaded next. Once a program is in memory, the scheduler is no longer concerned with it. Instead, that program's right to access the processor is determined by the operating system's processor manager.

Fig. 10.11   When a program first enters a multiprogramming system, a queuing routine copies it to a queue on a secondary storage device.

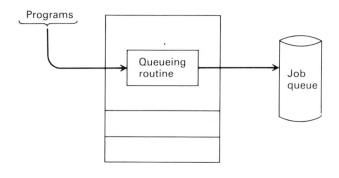

Fig. 10.12   Later, when space becomes available, the scheduling routine loads a program from the queue into main memory.

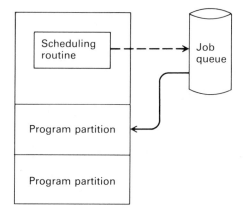

Spooling

The value of multiprogramming is that more programs can be run in the same amount of time. If the turnover rate of those programs can be increased, even greater efficiencies can be realized. For example, imagine a given system executes five concurrent programs, and that each program occupies memory for ten seconds. As soon as a program finishes executing, another one replaces it in memory. Thus, the computer can run thirty programs a minute. If we could reduce each program's run time to five seconds, we could run *sixty* programs in that same minute.

Picture a program that generates payroll for 1000 employees. Reading 1000 time cards takes at least two minutes. Printing 1000 checks takes a few minutes more, so the program will need at least four or five minutes to run. But what if the slow card reader and printer were replaced by a disk? A disk drive is much faster, so the program would run in much less time. Consequently, memory would be freed for another program much more quickly.

That's the essential idea behind **spooling**. Even with multiprogramming, it's common for all application programs to be waiting for I/O. When this happens, the processor has nothing to do. During these idle periods, the operating system's spooling module reads data from such slow devices as card readers or terminal keyboards and stores them on a high-speed medium such as disk, even before the program needing those data has been loaded into memory. Later, when the program *is* loaded, its input data can be read from disk. On output, data are spooled to disk and later dumped to the printer. Because the application program deals only with high-speed I/O, it finishes processing much more quickly, thus freeing space for another program.

Time-Sharing

Perhaps you have used a terminal to write original programs, execute existing software, or access data. Almost certainly, your terminal, along with dozens, even hundreds of others, was linked to a central computer. Such configurations often involve **time-sharing**.

Imagine a typical time-sharing application. Transactions—single program statements, lines of input data, or commands—are typed through a keyboard. In most cases, very little actual processing is required. Typing is slow; two transactions per minute is the best most people can do. To the computer, each user represents a string of brief, widely spaced processing demands. As a transaction is processed, the system knows that considerable time will pass before that user's next transaction is received, so the work space can be rolled out to secondary storage, making room for another application in main memory (*Fig. 10.13a*). Later, when the first user's next transaction arrives, his or her work space is rolled back in (*Fig. 10.13b*) and given control. On most time-shared systems, such **roll-in** and **roll-out** techniques are used to manage main memory space.

Imagine you have just spent twenty minutes typing the data for a statistical analysis program. Each data element was one brief transaction; your work to this point certainly fits the assumptions of a typical time-shared job. Your last transaction, however, is different. It's a command telling the system to process the data. It causes the computer to begin a computational routine that can easily run for two or three minutes. While your transaction is processed, every one of the other users on the system will have to wait, and that's intolerable.

The solution is **time-slicing**. Each program is restricted to a maximum "slice" of time, perhaps 0.01 second. If, during this interval, processing is completed, fine; control shifts to another program. If not, however, the long-running program is interrupted and moved to the end of the queue to await another turn. Time-slicing is the processor management technique used on a time-shared system.

Fig. 10.13 Roll-in and roll-out. When the system has finished processing a transaction, the user's work space is rolled out to disk (a). Later, the work space is rolled back in when the user's next transaction enters the system (b).

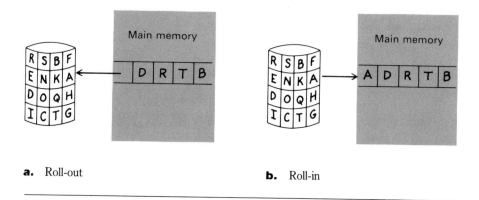

a. Roll-out   **b.** Roll-in

Multiprocessing

Multiprogramming and time-sharing require a resident operating system to deal with the conflicts that arise when multiple concurrent users share limited resources. Both techniques help to improve the efficiency of a system, allowing more programs to be processed over the same time period on the same hardware. However, the operating system modules, essential though they may be, occupy main memory and consume processor time; they represent unproductive overhead.

Consider, for example, the problem of controlling I/O. Channels were developed to relieve the processor of much of this responsibility. Unfortunately, a channel can't do the whole job itself; certain logical functions such as starting, finishing, and checking the status of the I/O operation were, until recently, performed by the main processor working under the control of the operating system. Why not identify the operating system code that performs these functions, and program a microprocessor to do the same things? We might replace the channel with this new I/O processor (*Fig. 10.14*). Now, because we have two *independent* processors, the instructions associated with I/O can be executed in parallel with more productive main processor activities. Two processors share the same main memory, forming a **multiprocessing** system.

If I/O control can be shifted to an independent processor, why not other functions (*Fig. 10.15*)? Near-future systems might contain several I/O processors, one to replace each channel. A database processor incorporating much of the logic of a database management system might control all communications with the database. For large scientific and engineering problems, an array processor might relieve the main processor of the time-consuming chore of array manipulation. Language processors might allow the direct execution of programs written in a high-level language, thus bypassing the inefficient compilation step. If many of the functions now associated with operating systems and system software are shifted to independent processors, these control programs (overhead) will no longer tie up the main processor's time. The result is greater efficiency.

Fig. 10.14   If a channel is replaced by an I/O processor, the main processor can be relieved of all responsibility for controlling I/O operations.

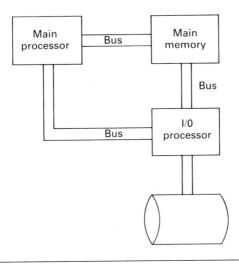

Fig. 10.15   In the near future, many overhead functions will be assigned to independent processors, thus freeing the main processor to work on application programs.

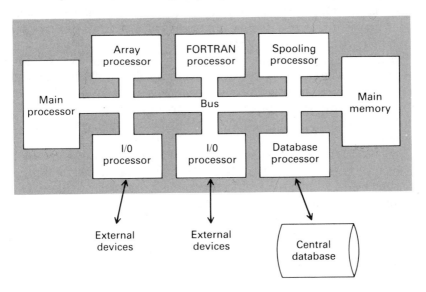

An interesting controversy concerns the future direction of the computer field—will small computers or big computers come to dominate? The answer is probably both. Almost by definition, multiprocessing systems are large, and yet major components, the secondary processors, are really microcomputers; in effect, small machines are used to construct bigger ones. In the next chapter, we'll study networks and discover another interesting marriage of large and small computer technologies.

Summary

A mainframe computer is much faster than its peripheral devices, and thus often spends more time waiting for I/O than processing data. One solution is multiprogramming. Two or more programs are loaded into main memory, and the processor executes them concurrently, switching its attention from one to the other. With multiple programs competing for the computer's limited resources, conflicts are inevitable. Most are resolved by the operating system.

One important operating system function is managing the processor's time. When an input or output operation begins, the operating system is notified through an interrupt. Given control, it places the program requesting I/O in a wait state and gives control of the processor to another program. Eventually, the end of the I/O operation is signaled by another interrupt. Once again, the operating system gets control, marks the appropriate program ready, and gives control back to an application program. The processor management module chooses the "next" program by using a priority algorithm.

The simplest form of memory management divides main memory into fixed-length partitions and loads one program in each one. Greater efficiency can be achieved by using dynamic memory management. With virtual memory management, programs are stored on disk, and only active portions are loaded into main memory. Another operating system module allocates peripheral devices to application programs.

When programs enter a multiprogrammed system, they are stored on a queue. Later, when memory space becomes available, a scheduler module selects the next program from the queue and loads it into main memory. To improve the turnover rate of programs, data are often spooled from slow-speed devices to disk, and then read from disk into the program. On output, results are spooled to disk and eventually dumped to the printer.

Time-sharing is often used on multiple terminal systems. Because the time between successive transactions is usually quite long, memory space can be managed by using roll-in and roll-out techniques. To eliminate the risk of one program tying up the system and forcing all other users to wait, time-slicing is used to manage the processor's time.

Under multiprocessing, two or more independent processors share a common memory. Multiprocessing can greatly reduce the processor time lost to nonproductive overhead functions.

Key Words

- concurrent
- dynamic memory management
- fixed partition memory management
- interrupt
- I/O device allocation

- memory management
- multiprocessing
- multi-programming
- operating system
- processor management
- queueing

- resource management
- roll-in/roll-out
- scheduling
- spooling
- time-sharing
- time-slicing
- virtual memory
- wait state

Self-Test

1. On what task does a typical computer spend most of its time?

   a. executing instructions
   b. compilation
   c. interpreting instructions
   d. waiting for I/O

2. With _____ , two or more programs are loaded into main memory and executed concurrently.

   a. multiprocessing
   b. multiprogramming
   c. compilation
   d. multitasking

3. A computer's resources are managed by its _____ .

   a. programmers
   b. hardware
   c. software
   d. operating system

4. The processor's time is allocated by _____ .

   a. hardware
   b. the operator
   c. software
   d. the operating system

5. An operating system can switch from program to program by responding to _____ .

   a. a program
   b. hardware
   c. the operator
   d. interrupts

6. The simplest type of memory management is _____ .

   a. block oriented
   b. fixed partition
   c. sector oriented
   d. dynamic

7. Under _____ memory management, each program is allocated as much memory as it needs.

a. dynamic   c. virtual
b. fixed   d. roll-in/roll-out

8. With _____ memory management, programs are stored on disk, and only active portions are loaded into memory.

a. dynamic   c. virtual
b. fixed partition   d. all of the above

9. As programs enter a multiprogramming system, they are stored on a _____ .

a. tape   c. queue
b. track   d. none of these

10. Programs are loaded into main memory by the operating system's _____ .

a. queueing routine   c. processor manager
b. memory manager   d. scheduler

11. Data are copied from a slow-speed device to a high-speed device for eventual input to a program with _____ .

a. scheduling   c. time-sharing
b. queueing   d. spooling

12. A system with a hundred or more terminals serviced by a central computer is probably a _____ system.

a. multiprogramming   c. multiprocessing
b. time-sharing   d. time-slicing

13. Most time-shared systems use _____ to manage memory.

a. fixed partitions   c. roll-in/roll-out
b. dynamic regions   d. pages

14. The processor management technique used on most time-sharing systems is _____ .

a. time-slicing   c. command processing
b. interrupt processing   d. none of the above

15. With _____ , two or more independent processors share the same memory.

a. multiprocessing

c. multicomputing

b. multiprogramming

d. multitasking

Answers

1.d   2.b   3.d   4.d   5.d   6.b   7.a   8.c   9.c   10.d   11.d   12.b   13.c   14.a   15.a

Relating the Concepts

1. Imagine that a computer's main memory contains only a single program. During input and output operations, the processor can do nothing. Why?

2. Briefly explain multiprogramming.

3. Distinguish between the terms simultaneous and concurrent. Why is this difference important?

4. Why is the operating system a good place to implement resource management?

5. What is an interrupt? Why are interrupts important to processor management on a multiprogrammed system?

6. On a virtual memory system, most of a given program is stored on a secondary device, and only active portions are actually loaded into main memory. Why is this important?

7. Distinguish between scheduling and spooling.

8. Processor management is concerned with the priority of programs already in main memory, while scheduling and queueing are concerned with the priorities of programs not yet in memory. Explain.

9. Briefly explain time sharing. How is memory space managed on a time-shared system? How is processor time managed?

10. Distinguish between multiprogramming and multiprocessing.

11.

Distributed Systems

KEY CONCEPTS

Data communication

Linking terminals and computers

Data communication software

Networks

Data Communication

On a time-shared system, users access a computer through terminals. Some terminals are **local**, linked directly to a computer by cables, while others are **remote**, communicating with distant computers over telephone lines or other transmission media. Remote computing involves a number of special problems. Let's investigate.

Within a computer, data are represented as discrete electrical pulses—0s and 1s. Since the system's components are normally within a few feet of each other, these bits can easily be moved from component to component. However, when we attempt to transmit electrical pulses over a distance, several things happen. First, the signal loses intensity or "dies down" because of the resistance of the wire (*Fig. 11.1*). At the same time, it picks up interference or **noise**; the static in the background of a distant radio station is a good example. The signal grows weaker and weaker as it moves away from its source, and the noise becomes more intense until eventually the signal is overwhelmed. If data are to be sent over a distance, the noise must be filtered out and the signal boosted occasionally.

Data are often transmitted in the context of a **carrier signal** such as the sine wave of *Fig. 11.2*. One complete "S-on-its-side" pattern is called a **cycle**. The height of the wave from the lowest to the highest point is its amplitude. The number of cycles per second is the wave's frequency. Because the carrier signal is transmitted with a known frequency and amplitude, it is possible to design equipment to filter and boost it.

How can these wave properties be used to encode and transmit binary data? Simple. Start with a standard wave of known amplitude and frequency, and let each cycle represent a single bit. To transmit a 1-bit, leave the wave alone; to transmit a 0-bit, vary the frequency of one cycle (*Fig. 11.3*). In other words, a normal cycle represents a 1-bit, and "something else," a 0-bit. The result is a continuous signal representing a pattern of bits.

Fig. 11.1   An electronic signal moving over a wire tends to lose intensity or die down due to the wire's resistance. Eventually, noise overwhelms the signal, and no data can be transmitted.

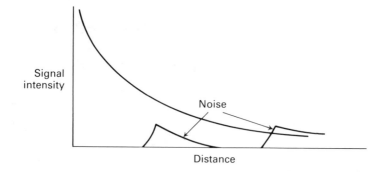

Fig. 11.2 Often, data are transmitted in the context of a carrier signal such as this sine wave.

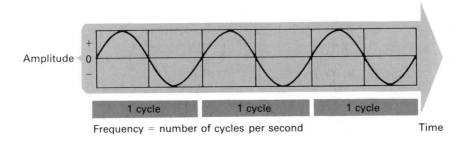

Frequency = number of cycles per second

Fig. 11.3 Binary data can be transmitted by selectively varying the carrier signal.

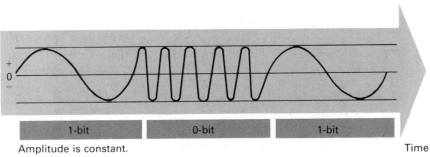

Amplitude is constant.   Time

The data are discrete electrical pulses. The wave is an **analog** representing the data. We use analogs every day. The height of a column of mercury in a thermometer isn't the actual temperature; it *represents* temperature. The position of a needle on your automobile's control panel isn't speed, but represents speed. A continuous wave passing over a communication line isn't the data, but it is analogous to the data.

Computers, however, do *not* store data as continuous waves; they store and manipulate discrete pulses. Because of this electronic incompatibility, whenever data are transmitted between a computer and a remote terminal, they must be converted from pulse form to wave form, and back again. Converting to wave form is called **modulation**; converting back is called **demodulation**; the task is performed by a hardware device called a **data set** or **modem** (modulator/demodulator). Normally, there is one at each end of a communication line (*Fig. 11.4*).

Fig. 11.4 A modem is used to modulate and demodulate a signal. Normally, there is a modem at each end of a data communication line.

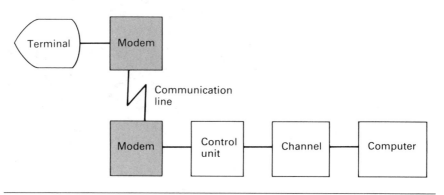

Many communication lines transmit analog signals because, until recently, we could not economically build equipment to deal with **digital** signals. Advances in electronics have made digital data transmission not only possible, but common; in fact, most new communication facilities are digital. With digital communication, there is no continuous carrier wave. Instead, bits are transmitted as brief, discrete pulses. These digital signals are less affected by noise, so data can be transmitted with greater accuracy.

The telephone network is probably the best known **data communication** medium. A typical voice-grade line is rated at roughly 2400 bits per second, or 2400 **baud**. High-speed, wide-band channels can transmit at rates approaching 1 million baud, and several baud rates between these two extremes are available. Microwave data transmission is an alternative to telephone lines. Unfortunately, microwave transmission is restricted to a "line of sight." The earth, as we all know, is round; it curves. This curvature limits the range of microwaves, making expensive relay stations or communication satellites necessary (*Fig. 11.5*).

We could spend considerable time discussing various communication media, but that would be needlessly confusing. Instead, we'll use a general term, **line**, to describe *any* data communication medium.

Fig. 11.5 Microwave data transmission is limited to a "line of sight." Long-distance microwave transmission requires relay stations or satellites.

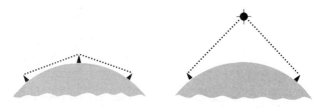

Linking Terminals and Computers

Imagine several terminals linked to a central computer. At the computer's end, data can be manipulated at speeds approaching several million characters per second. A typical 2400-baud line can transmit roughly 300 characters per second. What about the terminal? Given most people's typing speed, 10 characters per second is probably an exaggeration. We have a 10-character-per-second keyboard attached to a 300-character-per-second line which, in turn, is linked to a several million-character-per-second computer. That's quite a range!

A **buffer** big enough to hold a transaction or a full screen of data can help to synchronize the terminal and its communication line (*Fig. 11.6*). As the user types, the characters are stored in the buffer. When typing is completed, the user presses the enter key. In response to this signal, the contents of the buffer are transmitted over the line at the *line's* rated speed. On output, data move over the line and enter the buffer. From there they are displayed or printed at the *terminal's* rated speed. With a buffer in the middle, the speed disparity between the terminal and the line is bridged.

What happens at the other end of the line? A modern **transmission control unit**, often called a **front-end device**, is composed of a series of ports and associated buffers (*Fig. 11.6*). A **port** is a connection point for a communication line, and usually contains the electronics needed to modulate and demodulate the signal. Data enter the transmission control unit at a rate determined by the communication line, and move into the buffer associated with the "port of entry." Once all the data are in the buffer, the transmission control unit signals the channel which, in turn, signals the computer that data are ready to be input. As soon as the computer is ready, the data are transmitted over a bus line at the computer's internal processing speed. On output, data move to the control unit at computer speed, and are parceled out to the communication lines at much lower speeds.

Fig. 11.6   A terminal buffer helps to synchronize the speeds of the terminal and the line. At the computer's end, the transmission control unit contains a buffer for each port.

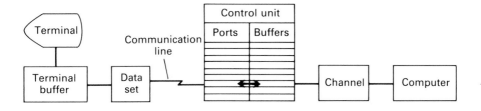

Data Communication Software

A typical time-shared system involves numerous terminals and communication lines linked to a computer through one or more front-end devices. Just coordinating all that hardware is difficult. Additionally, each terminal may support an independent user accessing an independent program. Data intended for program A are useless to program B; input and output must be routed to specific programs. Often, the operating system controls this hardware/software/data linkage through a process known as **polling**.

Start with a terminal. As data are typed, they enter the terminal's buffer. Finally, after the last character, the user presses enter. This turns on an electronic switch, marking the terminal "ready."

Now, move inside the computer. The operating system is in control, and has a table listing every active program and its associated terminal. Referring to this table, a polling signal is sent to the first program's terminal (*Fig. 11.7a*). In effect, the signal asks the terminal if it is ready to transmit data. We'll assume this user is still typing. Since the enter button has not yet been pressed, the ready switch is not on. Thus the operating system moves to the second program's terminal and issues another polling signal. This one is *our* terminal, and it's ready (*Fig. 11.7b*). Thus, the transaction is accepted and routed to our program (*Fig. 11.7c*).

Fig. 11.7   The computer polls terminals to determine which one will communicate with the computer next.

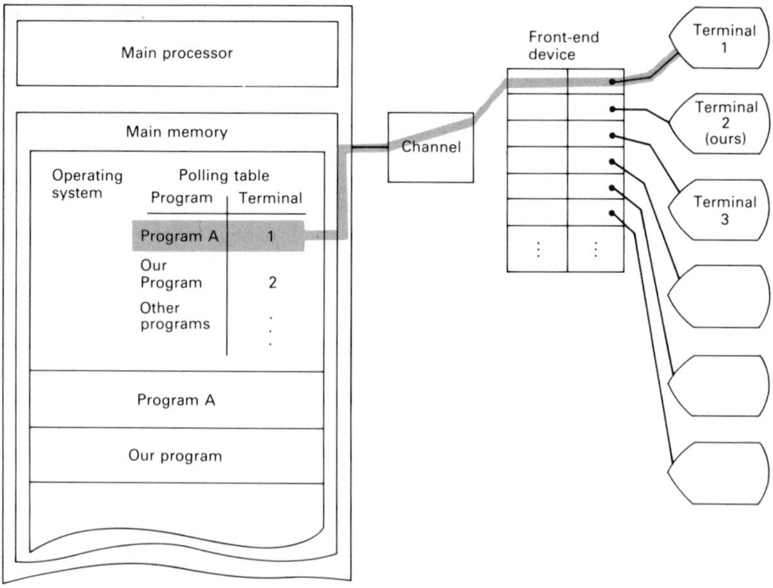

a.   A polling signal is sent to the terminal supporting the first program on the polling table.

Fig. 11.7

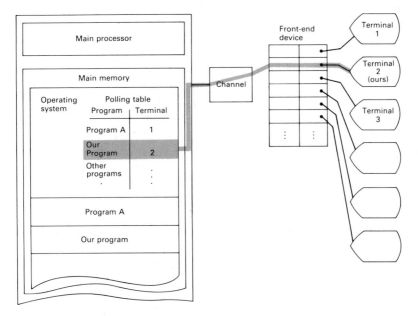

b. Since the first terminal is not yet ready, a polling signal is sent to the second program's terminal.

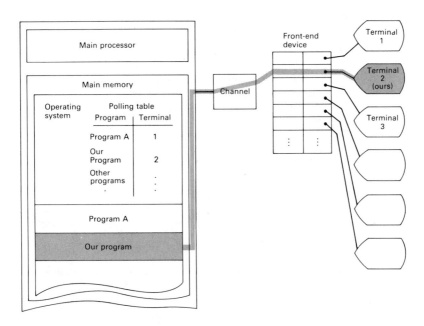

c. Since this terminal is ready, its data are read into the program.

A computer can do nothing without a program, and generating polling signals is no exception to that rule. Often, the polling routine is part of the operating system, but having the operating system generate the signals wastes a great deal of the main processor's valuable time. An option is giving the front-end device its own independent processor and assigning it responsibility for polling. On such systems, the front-end processor communicates directly with the terminals, continuously polling them, one by one. If a terminal is *not* ready, it is ignored until the next polling cycle; if a terminal *is* ready, its data are transferred into the front-end processor's buffer.

Inside the computer, the operating system (or another software module called a **data communication monitor**) must decide which program will get control next. Each program, remember, is associated with a particular front-end port. If a program's data have not yet reached its front-end buffer, there is no point giving that program control. Thus, the data communication monitor sends its own polling signal to the front-end processor asking, in effect, if data are in a given port's buffer. If the data have arrived, they are input, and the appropriate application program gets control. If not, the front-end device's next port is polled. Note that the mainframe communicates *only* with the front-end processor, and always at computer speed. The computer never has to wait for a terminal or a communication line. Instead, it is the less expensive front-end processor that waits for the slower system components to respond.

Networks

Historically, computers were so expensive that most large organizations did all their data processing on a single, centralized machine. While very efficient for such tasks as payroll and generating accounting reports, the centralized approach was not very useful to those who needed a quick response to a unique, local problem. With today's inexpensive micros and minis, there is no reason why a branch office, the engineering department, or any other group needing computer support cannot have its own computer. By linking these remote machines to a centralized computer via communication lines, local activity can be monitored and coordinated. This approach is called **distributed data processing**.

Note that distributed data processing involves a number of computers linked by communication lines. Generally, several independent computers linked by communication lines form a **network**.

Perhaps the best way to visualize a network is to consider an example. Let's use a computer-controlled supermarket checkout system. Each checkout station (*Fig. 11.8*) is equipped with a bar-code scanner. The checkout process begins when the clerk picks up a product, locates its Universal Product Code (UPC), and passes it over the scanner, which reads the code.

The checkout stations are attached to a minicomputer that controls access to a database containing, by Universal Product Code, the current selling price, description, inventory level, sales tax, and other data for each item in the store (*Fig. 11.9*). As a product code is scanned, it is input to the minicomputer, which locates the product on the database, adds the price and the sales tax to the customer's bill, and subtracts "1" from the product's inventory level. Next, the description, price, and tax are sent back to the checkout station, where a customer receipt is printed. This cycle continues until the entire order has been scanned. Because the scanning process is controlled by human beings, it is relatively slow, so the minicomputer can easily keep up with a dozen or more checkout stations.

Fig. 11.8 Supermarket checkout stations like this one scan the universal product code printed on most packages, and thus provide the basic input data to the supermarket network.

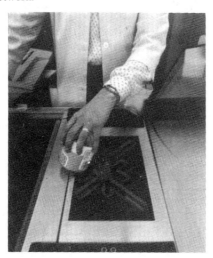

Fig. 11.9 When a universal product code is scanned, it flows into the store's minicomputer, which looks up the product's price, description, and other data in a database.

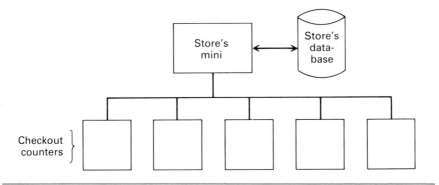

Although useful to the store, a computer-controlled supermarket checkout system's real value is improved control over warehousing and distribution. Generally, volume buying is cheaper than purchasing one item at a time. Thus, the supermarket chain buys products by the boxcar, stores them in a warehouse, distributes them to the individual stores, and sells them at a profit. Storing and distributing products can be expensive, however, and every penny spent on warehousing, shipping, or handling is a penny of potential profit lost. A successful supermarket chain keeps storage and distribution costs to a minimum.

With only a few products and only a few stores, the problem is simple. Consider, however, the number of products a typical supermarket carries. Multiply this by the number of stores in a chain, and try keeping track of all those products in all those stores. Techniques for solving such complex problems require a mainframe computer.

Thus, we add a third level to our supermarket network, a large, centralized mainframe (*Fig. 11.10*). The big machine is responsible for controlling inventory, both in the central warehouse and in all the stores. It also plans shipments to the stores. Data to support these applications are sent to the mainframe from the store minicomputers over communication lines.

Fig. 11.10   At the "top" of the supermarket network is a large mainframe that deals with inventory control and distribution.

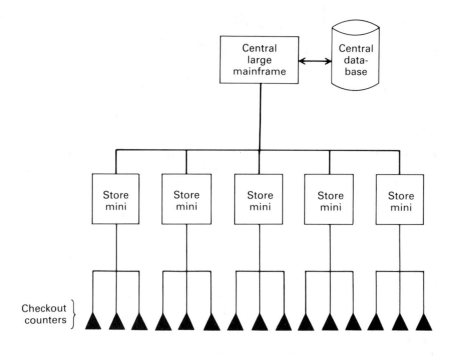

Fig. 11.11   Often, computers of similar power are linked to form a ring network. The communciation lines allow the computers to communicate with each other, and the network provides effective backup if one computer fails.

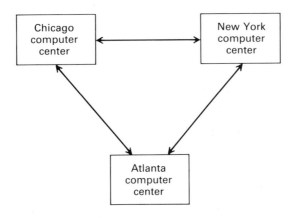

A network consists of several computers linked by communication lines. The machines can function independently, but their activities can also be coordinated. In the supermarket network, the checkout stations collect data, the minicomputers perform store-level processing, and the large mainframe handles chainwide inventory and distribution tasks. In another distributed network, the accounting, sales, production, and engineering departments of a business firm might have their own computers, with all the machines linked to a centralized mainframe housing the organization's database. With such a system, the individual departments have the flexibility to do their own processing, while the central machine ensures they use common data, and helps to monitor and control their activities.

Networks are not limited to such *hierarchical* structures, however. For example, many large organizations with computers spread all over the world link their machines to form a *ring* network (*Fig. 11.11*). Obviously, with all the computers linked, the various divisions and offices can exchange information. Less obvious is the backup provided by such a network; if one computer fails, its work can be switched to the others.

Not all networks are private. For example, anyone with a microcomputer, a modem, the right software, and a telephone can link to any number of computers and access a variety of data ranging from stock quotations, to library catalogs, to electronic bulletin boards. More sophisticated systems even allow users all over the world to exchange electronic mail. We have just begun to tap the potential of computer networks.

Summary

Cables link local terminals directly to a computer system. Remote terminals communicate with a computer over data transmission lines. Data are stored as discrete pulses inside a computer, but often must be converted to analog form for transmission over communication lines. Converting pulses to wave form is called modulation; converting back is called demodulation; the device that performs this function is a modem. Perhaps the best known data communication medium is the telephone network. Microwave transmission is an alternative.

There is a significant disparity in the speeds of terminals, communication lines, and computers. Buffers can help to synchronize such dissimilar devices or media. A computer can communicate with only one terminal at a time. It selects the "next" terminal through a polling process. Often, communication lines are attached to a computer system through a front-end device that assumes responsibility for polling terminals. The front-end device contains a port and a buffer for each line. Inside the computer, the operating system or a data communication monitor communicates with the front-end device, polling the ports to determine if a given program's data are in the buffer.

A network is a group of computers linked by communication lines. We used a supermarket checkout system to illustrate a hierarchical network. In a ring network, several computers of roughly equal power are linked, providing both communication and backup.

Key Words

- analog
- baud
- buffer
- carrier signal
- cycle
- data communication
- data communication monitor
- data set
- demodulation
- digital
- distributed data processing
- front-end device
- line
- local
- modem
- modulation
- network
- noise
- polling
- port
- remote
- transmission control unit

Self-Test

1. A _____ terminal communicates with a distant computer over data transmission lines.

   a. remote
   b. display
   c. printing
   d. local

2. The interference that distorts electronic signals transmitted over a distance is called _____ .

   a. static   c. noise
   b. interference   d. a spike

3. A wave is an example of _____ data.

   a. binary   c. digital
   b. transmitted   d. analog

4. Most new data transmission facilities are _____ .

   a. digital   c. analog
   b. microwave   d. none of the above

5. Inside a computer, data are stored as _____ .

   a. continuous waves   c. either
   b. discrete pulses   d. neither

6. A(n) _____ converts data from pulse form to wave form and back again.

   a. modem   c. channel
   b. control unit   d. interface

7. The basic measure of data communication speed is _____ .

   a. bits per second   c. characters per second
   b. bytes per second   d. baud rate

8. The general term _____ can be used to describe any data communication medium.

   a. network   c. line
   b. analog   d. digital

9. Devices or media that operate at different speeds can be synchronized by using a(n) _____ .

   a. line   c. buffer
   b. modem   d. data set

10. On a large computer, a number of communication lines can be linked to a single system through a(n) _____ .

   a. interface   c. minicomputer
   b. front-end device   d. bus line

11. A _____ is a connection point for a communication line.

   a. port   c. front end
   b. buffer   d. poll

12. A computer selects the terminal it will communicate with through a process known as _____ .

   a. compilation   c. dispatching
   b. interfacing   d. polling

13. Several computers linked by communication lines form a(n)
_____ .

   a. network   c. time-shared system
   b. distributed system   d. ring

14. The supermarket checkout system described in this chapter was an example of a _____ network.

   a. ring   c. hierarchical
   b. star   d. time-shared

15. A ring network configuration provides _____ .

   a. communication   c. both
   b. backup   d. neither

Answers

1.a   2.c   3.d   4.a   5.b   6.a   7.d   8.c   9.c   10.b   11.a   12.d   13.a   14.c
15.c

Relating the Concepts

1. Distinguish between local terminals and remote terminals.

2. Why is it necessary to filter and boost the signal when transmitting data over a distance?

3. What is a carrier signal? Why are carrier signals used?

4. Distinguish between analog and digital data.

5. What does a modem do? Why are modems necessary?

6. What is a buffer? Why are buffers used?

7. Briefly explain polling.

8. What is a front-end device? What functions are performed by a front-end device?

9. In Chapter 10, we discussed the idea of multiprocessing. Imagine a "highly intelligent" front-end processor that assumes responsibility for much of the data communication process. Would this be multiprocessing? Why, or why not?

10. What is a network?

Appendix

Number Systems

Decimal Numbers

A decimal number consists of a series of digits—0, 1, 2, 3, 4, 5, 6, 7, 8, 9—written in precise relative positions. The positions are important; for example, 23 and 32 are different numbers in spite of the fact that they contain the same two digits. The value of a given number is found by multiplying each digit by its place or positional value and adding the products. For example, the number 3582 represents:

$$
\begin{array}{rcr}
3 \text{ times } 1000 & = & 3000 \\
+5 \text{ times } 100 & = & 500 \\
+8 \text{ times } 10 & = & 80 \\
+2 \text{ times } 1 & = & 2 \\
\hline
& & 3582
\end{array}
$$

Generally, any number's value is simply the sum of the products of its digit and place values.

Take a close look at the decimal place values 1, 10, 100, 1000, 10000, and so on. The pattern is obvious. Rather than writing all those zeros, we can use scientific notation, for example, writing 10000 as 10^4. Because any number raised to the zero power is 1, we can write the decimal place values as our base (10) raised to a series of integer powers:

$$\ldots 10^8 \quad 10^7 \quad 10^6 \quad 10^5 \quad 10^4 \quad 10^4 \quad 10^2 \quad 10^1 \quad 10^0$$

A few general rules can be derived from our discussion of decimal numbers. First is the idea of place or positional value represented by the base (10) raised to a series of integer powers. The second is the use of the digit zero (0) to represent "nothing" in a given position. (How else could we distinguish 3 from 30?) Third, a total of ten digits (0 through 9) is needed to write decimal values. Finally, only values less than the base (in this case, 10) can be written with a single digit.

Binary Numbers

There is nothing to restrict the application of these rules to a base-10 number system. If the positional values are powers of 2, we have the framework of a binary, or base-2, number system:

$$\ldots 2^8 \quad 2^7 \quad 2^6 \quad 2^5 \quad 2^4 \quad 2^3 \quad 2^2 \quad 2^1 \quad 2^0$$

As in any number system, the digit zero (0) is needed to represent nothing in a given position. Additionally, the binary number system needs only one other digit, 1. Given these digit and place values, we can find the value of any number by multiplying each digit by its place value and adding these products. For example, the binary number 1100011 is:

$$
\begin{array}{rcl}
1 \text{ times } 2^6 &= 1 \text{ times } 64 = & 64 \\
+1 \text{ times } 2^5 &= 1 \text{ times } 32 = & 32 \\
+0 \text{ times } 2^4 &= 0 \text{ times } 16 = & 0 \\
+0 \text{ times } 2^3 &= 0 \text{ times } 8 = & 0 \\
+0 \text{ times } 2^2 &= 0 \text{ times } 4 = & 0 \\
+1 \text{ times } 2^1 &= 1 \text{ times } 2 = & 2 \\
+1 \text{ times } 2^0 &= 1 \text{ times } 1 = & \underline{1} \\
& & 99
\end{array}
$$

The decimal number 2 is 10 in binary; the decimal number 4 is 100. Decimal 5 is 101 (1 four, 0 twos, and 1 one).

Octal and Hexadecimal

Other number systems, notably octal (base 8) and hexadecimal (base 16) are commonly used with computers. The octal number system uses powers of 8 to represent positional values and the digit values 0, 1, 2, 3, 4, 5, 6, and 7. The hexadecimal number system uses powers of 16 and the digits 0, 1, 2, 3, 4, 5, 6, 7, 8, 9, A, B, C, D, E, and F. The hexadecimal number FF is:

$$15 \text{ times } 16^1 = 240$$
$$+\,15 \text{ times } 16^0 = \underline{15}$$
$$255$$

There are *no* computers that work directly with octal or hex values; a computer is a *binary* machine. These two number systems are used simply because it is easy to convert between them and binary. Each octal digit is exactly equivalent to three binary digits; each hexadecimal digit is exactly equivalent to four binary digits. Thus, octal and hex can be used as shorthand for displaying binary values.

Data Types

Numeric Data

Because binary numbers are so well suited to electronic devices, computers are at their most efficient when working with pure binary. A typical computer is designed around a basic unit of binary data called a word (usually 8, 16, or 32 bits). The high-order bit is usually set aside to hold a sign (0 for +, 1 for −); the remaining bits are data bits. There is no provision for a decimal point; decimal point alignment is the programmer's responsibility. For example, the biggest binary value that can be stored on a 32-bit word computer is

01111111111111111111111111111111

which is 2,147,483,647 in decimal, while the limit on a 16-bit machine is

0111111111111111

which is 32,767 in decimal.

Binary integers are fine for many applications, but at times, very large, very small, and fractional numbers are needed. With scientific notation, numbers are written as a decimal fraction followed by a power of 10; for example, the speed of light, 186,000 miles per second, is written as 0.186×10^6. Many computers can store and manipulate binary approximations of scientific numbers called real or floating-point numbers.

Certain applications, particularly business applications, demand precisely rounded decimal numbers. While any data type will do for whole numbers or integers, floating-point and binary numbers provide at best a close approximation to decimal fractions. Thus, many computers support a form of decimal data. Generally, computers are at their *least* efficient when processing decimal data.

String Data

Computers are not limited to storing and manipulating numbers, however; many applications call for such data as names, addresses, and product descriptions. These string values are typically stored as sets of individual characters, with each character represented by a code such as the ASCII or EBCDIC codes described in Chapter 2 (see Fig. 2.6). On many computers, a single coded character occupies one byte. Thus, the name "Jones" would be stored in five consecutive bytes.

It is important to note that strings and numbers are different. For example, if you type the digit 1 followed by the digit 2, each character will be stored as a 1-byte string in main memory. On a computer that uses the ASCII code, these two characters would appear as:

$$01010001 \quad 01010010$$

That's *not* the number 12. On a 16-bit computer, a pure binary 12 is stored as

$$0000000000001100$$

(Try using the digit-times-place-value rule.) Numbers and strings are different. That's why, in most programming languages, you must distinguish strings from numbers. The positional value of each digit in a number is significant. As we move from byte to byte, the positional values of the individual bits have no meaning in a string.

Data normally enter a computer through an input device in string form. Most computers have special instructions to convert strings to numbers. Arithmetic operations are performed on the numbers, and the results are converted back to string form before they are sent to an output device. Most programming languages perform these data type conversions for you; assembler languages are an exception.

Glossary

This glossary contains brief definitions intended to convey a sense of the meanings of selected key words. For more precise definitions see:

The American National Dictionary for Information Processing, American National Standards Institute, 1430 Broadway, New York, New York 10018.

The ISO Vocabulary of Data Processing, published by The International Standards Organization.

Access mechanism. On disk, the part that holds the read/write head. Like the tone arm on a stereo turntable, the access mechanism moves to position the read/write head over the track containing the desired data.

Access method. A software routine that translates a programmer's request for input or output into the physical commands required by the external device.

Address. A location in memory. Often, the bytes or words that make up memory are numbered sequentially; the byte's (or word's) number is its address.

Algorithm. A rule or a set of rules for arriving at an answer in a finite number of steps.

Analog. Data represented in a continuous physical form. The height of a column of mercury is an analog representation of a temperature. Computer data are transmitted over local telephone lines by converting them to continuous wave form. Contrast with digital.

Analysis. The step in the systems analysis and design process during which a systems analyst determines what must be done to solve a problem and develops a logical system plan.

Application program. A program written to perform an end user task. A payroll program or a computer game are application programs; an operating system is not.

Architecture. See Computer architecture.

Arithmetic and logic unit. The part of a computer's processor that executes instructions.

Array. A data structure in which memory is allocated as a series of numbered cells. Individual data elements can be placed in or extracted from one of these cells by referring to the cell's number or numbers.

Assembler. A programming language in which one mnemonic source statement is coded for each machine-level instruction.

Backup. Extra hardware, software, or data intended to keep a computer system running in the event that one or more components fail.

Base. In a number system, the number used to define positional values. For example, decimal uses base 10, while binary uses 2 as its base.

Batch processing. A type of computer application in which data are collected over time and then processed together. For example, payroll data might be collected throughout the week and processed on Friday. Contrast with Transaction processing.

Baud. The basic unit of data communication speed measured in discrete signal events per second. Since the basic unit of data transmitted is a bit, a baud rate usually measures bits per second.

Binary. A base 2 number system that uses values 0 and 1.

Bit. A binary digit.

Board. See Circuit board

Boot. A small routine, read into main memory when the computer is turned on, which reads the rest of the operating system into memory. See also Initial program load.

Buffer. Temporary storage used to compensate for the different speeds of adjacent devices.

Bug. An error in a program.

Bus. A set of parallel wires used to transmit data, commands, or power.

Byte. Eight bits. On many computer systems, the smallest addressable unit of main memory.

Cable. An electrical connector; often, a shielded, serial wire.

Carrier signal. A standard, predictable signal, such as a sine wave, used to transmit data. The unaltered signal indicates an absence of data; alterations in the standard pattern convey meaning.

Cassette, or **magnetic cassette.** An inexpensive secondary storage medium. Standard cassette tape.

Central processing unit. See Processor.

Channel. A device used to attach input, output, and secondary storage devices to a large computer system. The channel contains its own processor, and thus can free the main processor from responsibility for controlling I/O operations.

Character. A single letter, digit, or other symbol. On many computers, each byte of memory can hold a single character in coded form.

Chip. A tiny square of silicon that holds thousands of integrated electronic circuits.

Circuit board. A flat surface on which chips are linked by electronic paths embedded in the surface. Examples include processor boards, memory boards, and interface boards.

Clock. A device that generates the regular electronic pulses that drive a computer.

Code. (1) A set of rules for representing characters as bit patterns. (2) To write a program.

Command. (1) A control signal that tells a hardware component to perform a specific function. For example, a fetch command tells memory to transfer the contents of a single memory location to a bus, while a seek command tells a disk interface to position the access mechanism. (2) A request from a programmer, an operator, or a user to an operating system asking that a specific function be performed. For example, a request to load a program.

Command language. A language

for communicating with an operating system.

Command processor. An operating system module that reads, interprets, and carries out commands.

Communication interface. A device that links a communication line to a computer system.

Compiler. A support program that reads a source program, translates the source statements to machine language, and outputs a complete binary object program.

Computer. A machine that processes data into information under control of a stored program.

Computer architecture The physical structure of a computer; in particular, the way in which a computer's components are linked together.

Computer program. A series of instructions that guides a computer through some process.

Concurrent. Over the same time period.

Console. A device, often a keyboard/display unit, through which an operator communicates with a computer.

Contiguous. Next to; adjoining.

Continuous. Unbroken; connected. Contrast with Discrete.

Control unit, instruction. See Instruction control unit.

Control unit, I/O. An electronic device that links an I/O device to a channel.

CPU. Acronym for Central processing unit.

Cursor. The blinking line or box that indicates where the next character typed or output will appear on a display screen.

Cycle. Any set of operations repeated regularly in the same order. In data communications, one complete "S-on-its-side" sine wave represents a single cycle.

Cylinder. On a multisurface disk pack, one position of the access mechanism, which defines a set of several tracks.

Data. Raw, unstructured, unprocessed facts.

Database. A collection of related data. Generally, an integrated, centralized collection of an organization's data.

Database management system. Software and/or hardware that controls access to a database.

Data communication. Transmitting data over a communication line.

Data communication monitor. A software routine or program that controls or monitors the data communication process.

Data dependency. A condition that occurs when a program's logic is excessively dependent on its physical data structure. Data-dependent programs are difficult to maintain.

Data dictionary. A collection of data about the data that are processed by a system.

Data element. A single, meaningful unit of data.

Data flow diagram. A graphic representation of a logical system showing how data flow between sources, processes, stores, and destinations.

Data management. Storing data in such a way that they can be retrieved when needed.

Data processing. Converting data into information.

Data set. See modem.

Data structure. An organized set of data. Examples include a list, an array, and a file.

Debug. To remove errors (bugs) from a program.

Declarative language. See Nonprocedural language.

Demodulation. The reverse of modulation. To convert data from analog to digital form.

Design. The step in the systems analysis and design process during which an analyst develops a physical design for the system.

Digital. Data represented as individual, discrete digits. Contrast with analog.

Direct access. Accessing data without regard for its physical position in a file or on disk. Contrast with Sequential access.

Directory. See Index. The term directory is generally used to mean the list of files stored on a disk or some other secondary medium. Index is a more general term.

Discrete. Opposite of continuous. Separate; independent.

Disk, magnetic. A flat, platelike surface on which data can be stored magnetically.

Disk pack. A set of two or more disks stacked on a common drive shaft and accessed by a common set of read/write heads.

Diskette. A thin, flexible magnetic disk often used on small computer systems.

Display, or **display screen.** A TV-like screen that displays data.

Distributed data processing. A technique for using computers in which several machines are used for local data processing activities and are linked to a central computer that often houses the organization's database. Such a configuration provides many of the advantages of decentralization without sacrificing the advantages of centralization.

Documentation. Diagrams, comments, and other materials that explain or clarify a program.

Dynamic memory management. Allocating memory space to application programs as the space is needed.

Execution. The act of carrying out an instruction or performing a routine.

Execution time, or **E-time.** The time during which an instruction is executed by the arithmetic and logic unit.

Feasibility study. A study performed early in the system analysis and design process and aimed at determining if the problem can be solved.

Fetch. To locate a unit of data or an instruction in main memory and send it, over a bus, to the processor.

Fiber optics. A data communication medium on which laser light pulses are transmitted over a glass fiber cable.

Field. A single, meaningful data element in a file.

File. A collection of related records.

Fixed partition memory manage-

ment. A memory management technique in which the available memory space is divided into several fixed-length partitions, and one program is loaded into each partition.

Floppy disk. See Diskette.

Flowchart. A graphic representation of a program in which symbols represent logical steps and flowlines define the sequence of those steps.

Fourth-generation language. See Nonprocedural language.

Front-end device. A transmission control unit that links a number of communication lines to a computer system. Often, the front-end device contains enough intelligence to assume responsibility for polling terminals.

Graphics. Computer output in the form of points, lines, and shapes.

Hard disk. A rigid disk. Contrast with floppy disk, or Diskette. Generally, a hard disk spins constantly; consequently, data access is much faster than with diskette. Also, hard disk has a greater data storage capacity.

Hardware. Physical equipment. Contrast with Software.

Hierarchy chart. A tool for modeling a computer program as a hierarchy of single-function modules.

Implementation. The step in the systems analysis and design process during which programs are written, hardware selected and installed, operating procedures written, and so on. Implementation ends with the release of the program or system to a user.

Index. A list of the contents of a disk pack or other storage medium showing the locations of each file or program. More generally, a value or set of values, such as an index register or a subscript, used to locate specific data elements.

Information. The meaning a human being assigns to data. Processed data.

Information processing. See Data processing.

Initial program load, or **IPL.** The process of loading the operating system when the computer is first turned on. Big systems are IPLed; small systems are booted.

Input. Transferring data from an external device into a computer's main memory.

Input/output control system, or **IOCS.** The operating system module that assumes responsibility for communicating directly with input, output, and secondary storage devices.

Instruction. One step in a program. Each instruction tells the computer to perform one of its basic functions.

Instruction control unit. The part of a computer's processor that decides which instruction will be executed next.

Instruction counter. A special register that holds the address of the next instruction to be executed.

Instruction register. A special register that holds the instruction being executed by the processor.

Instruction set. The electronic circuits that add, subtract, multiply, divide, copy, compare, request input, and request output. On most computers, these are the circuits that make up the arithmetic and logic unit.

Instruction time, or **I-time.** The time during which the next instruction is fetched from main memory and interpreted by the processor's instruction control unit.

Integrated circuit memory. Memory composed of integrated circuit chips.

Interface. On a small computer, an electronic component, often a board, that links an external device to a computer. More generally, an electronic component that links two different devices.

Interpreter. A support program that reads a single source statement, translates that statement to machine language, executes those machine-level instructions, and then moves on to the next source statement. Contrast with Compiler.

Interrupt. An electronic signal that causes a computer to stop what it is doing and transfer control to the operating system in such a way that the task being performed at the time of the interrupt can later be resumed.

I/O. Input/output.

I/O control unit. See Control unit, I/O.

I/O device allocation. The task (usually performed by the operating system) of allocating input, output, and secondary storage devices to application programs.

IPL. See Initial program load.

K. When referring to memory or to secondary storage capacity, 1024 bytes or words.

Keyboard. An input device on which characters are represented as discrete keys. When a key is pressed, the associated character is input to the computer system.

Library. A collection of related files or programs.

Line. A communication medium connecting two or more points.

Linkage editor. A system program that combines object modules to form a load module, outputs the load module to a library, and then loads the program into main memory.

List structure. A list of data elements separated by commas, semicolons, or some other separator character.

Load module. A complete machine-level program in a form ready to be loaded into main memory and executed.

Loader. A system program that combines object modules to form a load module, and then loads the program into main memory. Similar to a linkage editor, except that a loader does not output the load module to a library.

Local. Connected to a computer by regular electric wires. In close proximity to the computer. Contrast with Remote.

Logical I/O. Input or output operations performed without regard for the physical structure of the data. Under traditional data management, a request for a logical record.

Logical system. A system design that focuses on *what* must be done, but not on *how* to do it.

Machine cycle. The basic operating

cycle of a processor during which a single instruction is fetched, interpreted, and executed.

Machine language. Binary instructions that can be stored in main memory, fetched, and executed by a computer.

Magnetic disk. See Disk, magnetic.

Magnetic drum. A cylinder coated on the outside surface with a magnetic material. Data are stored around the outer surface and accessed by a series of read/write heads, one head per track. A very fast medium with limited storage capacity. The first significant secondary storage medium.

Magnetic media. Input, output, or secondary storage media that represent data as magnetic patterns.

Magnetic tape. A popular backup medium. A ribbon of mylar coated with magnetic material. Data are recorded along the tape's surface.

Mainframe. The processing unit of a large computer system, or the processing unit plus other components contained in the same physical cabinet as the processing unit of a large computer system.

Main memory, or **Main storage.** Memory that can be directly accessed by the processor.

Main processor. On a multiprocessing computer, the primary processor. Sometimes used as a synonym for Processor.

Maintenance. Continuing support of a program or a system after it has been released.

Memory. The computer component in which instructions and data are stored.

Memory board. A circuit board that holds memory chips.

Memory management. Allocating main memory space to application programs, a task usually performed by the operating system.

Message-switching. Routing messages by receiving, storing, and forwarding them.

Microcomputer. A small computer system. A typical microcomputer is composed of a microprocessor, main memory, and one or more input/output devices.

Microprocessor. A processor on a single integrated circuit chip. The processor in a microcomputer system.

Microsecond. One millionth of one second.

Microwave. An electromagnetic wave that is used to transmit data.

Millisecond. One thousandth of one second.

Minicomputer. A small, digital computer, smaller than a mainframe but bigger than a microcomputer.

Modem. An acronym for MOdulator-DEModulator. A device that converts data from the computer's internal digital form to analog wave form, and back again. Used to link computer equipment to a telephone line.

Modulation. Converting data from digital form to analog wave form.

Monitor. See Display.

Motherboard A metal or plastic framework that holds a computer's circuit boards. Often, circuit boards slide into slots on the framework, and are electronically linked by bus lines.

MS/DOS. A popular microcomputer operating system.

Multiple-bus architecture. A computer architecture in which more than one bus line is used to link components. Often, separate bus lines are provided for commands, addresses, and data. Often, independent bus lines link the main processor and main memory, the channel processors and the main processor, and the channel memories and main memory.

Multiprocessing. Two or more independent processors sharing a common memory.

Multiprogramming. One computer concurrently executing several programs.

Nanosecond. One billionth of one second.

Network. Two or more computers linked by communication lines.

Noise. In data communications, electronic interference.

Nonprocedural language. A programming language in which the programmer simply describes the logical structure of a problem instead of writing a procedure to solve it. Also called a fourth-generation language or a declarative language.

Nonvolatile memory. Memory that maintains its contents even when power is lost. Secondary storage is nonvolatile; random access memory (RAM) is typically volatile.

Object module. A machine-level translation of a programmer's source code.

Open. To prepare a file for processing. For example, opening a file on disk involves checking the index to find the track and sectors where the file's data are stored.

Operand. The portion of an instruction that specifies the registers and/or memory locations that are to participate in the operation.

Operating system. A collection of program modules that control the operation of the computer. A typical operating system allocates resources, schedules programs, controls access to input and output devices, and manages data.

Operation code. The portion of an instruction that specifies the operation to be performed; e.g., add, subtract, etc.

Optical media. Generally, input media on which data are represented as light and dark patterns that can be interpreted by an optical scanner.

Output. The act of transferring data or information from the computer's main memory to an external device.

Packaged software. Purchased programs. Programs obtained in finished, ready-to-use form. Contrast with customized software or original software.

Packet switching. A data transmission technique in which a message is broken into discrete, digital packets. The packets are then transmitted independently over a high-speed line, and the message is reassembled at the other end.

Parallel. Side by side. Parallel processing involves performing two or more tasks at the same time. Parallel data transmission involves sending bits, side by side, over parallel wires. Contrast with Serial.

Parity bit. In memory, an extra bit appended to the data bits, that allows a computer to check the bit pattern for accuracy.

Peripheral hardware. Input, output, and secondary storage devices attached to a computer system.

Personal computer. A small, inexpensive microcomputer system marketed for use by individuals.

Physical I/O. The act of transferring a physical block of data to or from a peripheral device. For example, on diskette, each physical I/O operation might transfer one sector; on a printer, each physical I/O operation might transfer one line.

Physical system. A system design that identifies specific physical components, such as computer programs, input and output devices, secondary storage devices, other hardware, data files, data flows, media, and procedures.

Picosecond. One millionth of one millionth of a second.

Pixel. A picture element. A spot on a display screen that can be selectively turned on or off. The basic unit of a graphic display.

Polling. Asking a series of terminals, or checking a series of buffers, one by one, to see if they have data to transmit. A technique for determining who gets to transmit data next.

Port. The point at which a communication line enters a computer system.

Primitive command. A machine-level hardware command; e.g., a fetch command whereby a processor requests data from main memory, or a seek command whereby a disk interface is told to position the access mechanism.

Printer. A device that outputs printed characters.

Problem definition. The first step in the programming and/or systems analysis and design process during which the programmer or the analyst defines the problem

Processing. (1) Executing instructions. (2) Converting data into information.

Processor. The component of a computer that selects and executes instructions. The processor contains a clock, an instruction control unit, an arithmetic and logic unit, and registers.

Processor management. The task of allocating the processor's time to application programs. Usually performed by the operating system.

Program. See Computer program.

Programmer. A person who writes computer programs.

PROM. Programmable read-only memory.

Prompt. A brief message printed or displayed by a program or by the operating system asking the user to provide input.

Protocol. A set of rules for establishing communication between two devices.

Punched card. An input medium that represents data as patterns of holes punched in a card.

Queueing. Placing application programs on a waiting line (or queue) for eventual loading into main memory.

RAM (random access memory). Memory that can be directly addressed, read, and written by the programmer. The main memory of a computer is generally RAM. Contrast with ROM.

Random access. See Direct access.

Read/write head. The component that transfers data to or from the surface of disk or magnetic tape.

Record. A collection of related fields. For example, all the fields related to an employee's pay would constitute that employee's payroll record; all the fields related to a student's academic performance would constitute that student's academic history record.

Redundant data. Data that are repeated in two or more places.

Register. Temporary storage used to hold data, instructions, or control information in the processor. Often, the current instruction, the data being manipulated by that instruction, and key control information are stored in registers.

Relative address. An address relative to a reference point; for example,

the tenth byte away from the beginning of a program, or the third record in a file.

Relative record number. The location of a record relative to the beginning of a file; for example, the fourth record in a file. Given the actual track and sector of the first record in the file, it is possible to compute the address of any other record given its relative record number.

Remote. Distant. Linked to a computer via communication lines. Contrast with Local.

Resolution. A measure of the precision or sharpness of a graphic image. Often, a function of the number of pixels on a screen.

Resource management. An operating system responsibility on many large, multiprogrammed computer systems. Often includes managing such resources as processor time, main memory space, and access to secondary storage devices.

Roll-in/roll-out. A memory management technique used on time-shared systems in which programs are rolled out to secondary storage in between transactions and then rolled back into main memory when a transaction arrives.

ROM (read-only memory). A type of memory that cannot be modified by the programmer.

Rotational delay. On disk or drum, the time required for the desired sector to rotate to the read/write head after the head has been positioned over the desired track.

Routine. A program module.

Scheduling. Determining which program will be loaded into main memory when space becomes available. A task usually performed by the operating system.

Secondary storage. Nonvolatile memory such as disk or magnetic tape used for the long-term storage of program instructions and data. Generally, the data and instructions currently being processed by a computer are stored in main memory; all other data and instructions are stored in secondary storage.

Sector. A fixed-length element of disk or other magnetic storage that holds a single physical record. A common sector length on microcomputer systems is 512 characters.

Security. Software, hardware, and procedural elements that are intended to protect or safeguard computer equipment, data, or programs.

Seek time. The time needed to position a disk's access mechanism over a specific track.

Sequential access. Accessing records in a fixed order, generally, the order in which they are physically recorded.

Serial. One by one. Contrast with Parallel. Serial data transmission involves sending a stream of bits, one after another, over the same wire.

Single-bus architecture. A computer architecture in which all internal components are linked by a single bus line.

Slot. On a motherboard, one of several openings into which a circuit board can be plugged.

Software. Programs. Contrast with Hardware.

Source code. Program instructions written in a source language such as BASIC, COBOL, FORTRAN, or Pascal.

Spooling. On input, transferring data to secondary storage and holding them for eventual processing. On output, transferring data to secondary storage for eventual output to an output device. A technique used to make batch processing applications more efficient.

Storage. Memory.

Stored program. A series of instructions placed in a computer's main memory to control that computer. Distinguishes a computer from a calculator.

System. A group of components that function together to achieve an objective.

System flowchart. A graphic representation of a physical system in which symbols represent programs, hardware components, files, and so on.

System software. Support software;

for example, the operating system. Contrast with Application program.

Systems analysis. The process of converting a user's needs into a working system.

Systems analyst. A professional who translates user needs into the technical specifications needed to implement a system.

Telecommunication. Transmitting signals over distances by means of telephone lines, radio signals, or other media.

Terminal. Hardware placed at the entry or exit point of a communication network for the purpose of entering or obtaining data.

Time-sharing. A series of techniques that allows multiple users, each controlling an independent terminal, to share a single computer. Roll-in/roll-out is a common memory management technique. Time-slicing is a common processor management technique. Access to terminals is often controlled by polling.

Time-slicing. A processor management technique in which an application program is given a discrete "slice" of time in which to complete its work. If the work is not completed during a single time slice, the program loses control of the processor and must return to the end of the queue to await another turn.

Token. An electronic signal, often part of a protocol. See Token-passing network.

Token-passing network. A communication network in which the right to transmit is determined by an electronic signal called a token that is passed from terminal to terminal. Only the terminal holding the token can transmit data over the line.

Track. One of a series of concentric circles around which data are stored on disk or drum. Tracks are often subdivided into sectors.

Transaction. An exchange between a user and a computer that accomplishes a single logical function. For example, all the steps involved in requesting cash from an automatic teller machine constitute a single transaction.

Transaction processing. Processing transactions as they occur, rather than in a batch. Contrast with Batch processing.

Transmission. Sending data from one location to another over a communication line.

Transmission control unit, or **TCU.** A control unit that links a transmission line or lines to a computer system.

User. A person or group that uses a program or a system.

Video disk. A secondary storage medium that records and reads data using a laser beam.

Virtual memory. A memory management technique in which only active portions of a program are actually loaded into main memory.

Voice I/O. The input or output of spoken sounds.

Volatile memory. Memory that loses its content when the power is turned off.

Wait state. A condition whereby a given task or process must await the completion of an event before it can resume.

Winchester disk. A type of magnetic disk on which the disk surface or surfaces are packaged together with their own set of read/write heads. Popular on microcomputer systems.

Word. The basic storage unit around which a computer system is designed. On all but the smallest microcomputers, a word consists of two or more bytes.

Index